The
NO-SUGAR!
Desserts & Baking
Cookbook

The
NO-SUGAR!
Desserts & Baking
Cookbook

Over 65 delectable yet healthy sugar-free treats

YSANNE SPEVACK
PHOTOGRAPHY BY NICKI DOWEY

LORENZ BOOKS

CONTENTS

Let's Go No-Sugar! **6**

  Let's Go Light! **8**

  Why Go No-Sugar? **11**

  No-Sugar Sweeteners **13**

Hot Puddings, Crumbles and Custard **24**

Jellies, Mousses and Soufflés **40**

Ice Cream, Snow Cones and Ice Pops **60**

Tarts, Pies and Cheesecakes **74**

Special Occasion Cakes **110**

Cupcakes, Slices and Scones **136**

Biscuits, Cookies and Confections **164**

  Nutritional Notes **186**

  Index **189**

  Acknowledgements **192**

Let's go No-Sugar!

I've thought a lot about entertaining and what makes the food special: healthy main dishes, warming soups, crisp salads... yes! But it's the dessert that separates an excellent home-cooked meal from something really memorable. Dessert has the power to transform a dinner into a dinner party, make your guests feel celebrated, and let them know that this is not just a regular supper.

I'm British, but I've lived in Los Angeles and New York for more than a decade. It's become a wonderful challenge to make inclusive desserts for all of my guests, from the guy who loves sweet sugary stuff, to the fashionable ladies who strive to be conscious of their diets. I've tried and tested all of these desserts over many years, so that everyone at the table can enjoy my dishes without any sense of deprivation for the sugar-worshippers, and with total guilt-free indulgence for the more abstemious and healthy eaters.

I love making California-style raw desserts with superfoods like raw cacao and goji berries, baking New York-style cupcakes that are miraculously as luxuriously sweet and creamy as the sugar-laden versions, as well as traditional British-style puddings that are hearty and comforting for one and all.

In this book, I've also included simple recipes that make good things for lunch boxes, quick sugar-free desserts for weeknights, sugar-free ice pops and ice creams for summer months, and hot puddings for those days in winter when there's nothing better than a cup of tea and a bowl of nostalgia. Christmas classics and teatime treats have been reimagined to exclude sugar, as well as pies, scones, cookies, confections and some pretty gorgeous birthday cakes.

Many of these recipes are gluten-free or low-gluten, vegan and dairy free, and of course, every single recipe is free from sugar. Enjoy these kind and delicious desserts and let's go no-sugar!

Ysanne Spevack

Let's Go Light!

Lower gluten, lower dairy and zero sugar. That's how many people want to eat on a daily basis – not restricted, with a little joy and delight in our diets, but with fewer unhealthy ingredients. This collection includes recipes that are naturally sweeter because they're fruit based; some raw recipes; and other recipes that are traditional baked treats remixed to include some of the new sugar alternatives. Most of these recipes can be enjoyed by children and adults alike. Some are paleo-friendly and raw vegan, but also lots of them are more family oriented, with plenty of dairy, eggs and wheat.

MY NO-SUGAR PHILOSOPHY

This book will help you remove all refined sugar from your own diet and to wean your family off sugar too. My philosophy is to create sweet, healthy, delicious desserts using nutritious ingredients that aren't highly processed or refined and that are rich in minerals, phytonutrients and flavour.

To be clear, this book defines sugar as the stuff that's sold in bags with the word 'sugar' printed on the front. Many of these recipes do contain simple carbohydrates that naturally raise the blood's glucose content, for example honey, so diabetics should consult a physician before using this book. That said, many of these desserts can be eaten safely by Type-1 diabetics and many of them are as low-calorie as they are tooth-friendly.

For me, avoiding refined sugar isn't just about lowering the negative impact of glucose on the blood – it's about raising the positive impact of the things we use instead, in this golden age of nutritious, organic, unprocessed ingredients.

It's about eating for a better mood and more energy throughout the day and feeding your kids food that supports excellent behaviour that will help them to concentrate, grow and thrive.

It's about supporting health at every level, for better sleep and clearer skin, greater awareness and intuition, to help prevent illnesses and improve fertility. It's about eating foods that are rich in minerals and excite the palate, and never having a guilty internal dialogue with yourself about having eaten something you know will make you feel bad.

It's about saying yes to more flavour and delight in your dessert not as an alternative, but as an automatic choice, and vowing never to own a bag of sugar again, but without any complaints from your friends and family because... they don't even notice!

LET'S EAT SWEET, BUT BETTER!

We are fortunate to live in a time when we can enjoy ingredients originating in every corner of the beautiful world, but sometimes it's tricky to know what to do with them.

I've used many different kinds of no-sugar sweeteners in these recipes, including some ingredients your grandmother would recognize and some that she wouldn't.

Some of these recipes include natural and unprocessed sweeteners that have only recently become available in the West, but are time-honoured and loved in the places they originate and are now starting to be grown locally to you.

Of course, this is nothing new; adventurers have mixed and matched new ingredients from the spice route with European produce since the first boat

It's about eating for a better mood and more energy throughout the day and feeding your kids food that that will help them to concentrate, grow and thrive

My philosophy is to create sweet, healthy, delicious desserts using nutritious ingredients that aren't highly refined or processed

set sail. One of the reasons we began to travel is to attempt to satiate our desires for new, innovative tastes and to bring them back to our homelands to grow in our gardens.

Some of these recipes rely only on the natural sugars in familiar fruits and vegetables. Macerate fruit, roast vegetables, soak seeds and suddenly, familiar ingredients become sugar-free sweeteners using old-fashioned techniques.

Honey is forbidden by some as being too high on the glycaemic index, but it has a treasured place in my own sugar-free sweeteners pantheon due to the beautifully complex flavours and consistencies, as well as the incredibly rich health-properties of organic, local bee products and the magical royal jellies, pollens and waxes of the hive.

Many of these recipes were developed from scratch and even those that were originally based on traditional, sugar-containing recipes have been thought through carefully, choosing a particular combination of no-sugar sweeteners specially for each dish.

With most natural sweeteners, it's good to be informed so you can make better choices about which ones to use – and they do vary widely in quality from one brand to the next. I've shared my favourite brands and varieties of all these ingredients so you can make your own informed choices about what you're happy to eat and decide whether there are any of these ingredients you'd rather keep for infrequent, occasional use rather than eating every week.

Macerate fruit, roast vegetables, soak seeds and suddenly, familiar ingredients become sugar-free sweeteners using old-fashioned techniques

Why Go No-Sugar?

Numerous peer-approved medical scientific studies have shown that sugar consumption above 25g/1oz per day is linked to diabetes, obesity, heart disease, inflammatory diseases, immunity dysfunction and depression.

This is why the World Health Organization recommends that adults get no more than 5% of their calories from refined sugar, which is about 25g/1oz per day, or roughly 6 teaspoons. In the UK, the average consumption is currently about 50g/2oz per day for adults and about 75g/3oz for teenagers – three times the amount of refined sugar that scientists recommend.

In the USA, the average adult consumes about 200g/8oz of refined sugar per day – eight times more sugar every day than the World Health Organization recommends as safe.

The World Health Organization is a conservative body of experts, not known for giving radical health advice. Their recommendations are considered and are backed up by extensive scientific medical research.

Although eating too much sugar is proven to be bad for your health, many sugar substitutes also have their own drawbacks, especially those created artificially in a laboratory. The most widely used artificial sweetener is aspartame. Aspartame has been linked to several health issues, including its effect on the brain that makes dieters crave food. It turns off the brain's natural hormonal responses that make you feel satisfied and stop eating, so that if a dieter consumes a canned drink that contains aspartame, there is a risk that they'll keep eating more food than they would if they'd consumed a drink

With most natural sweeteners, it's good to be informed so you can make better choices about which ones to use — and they do vary widely in quality from one brand to the next

It's a very good idea to avoid sugar, but I'll show you how to replace it in homemade desserts healthily, in a balanced way, with practical home kitchens and a busy modern lifestyle in mind

containing refined sugar. Aspartame has been linked to cancers like lymphoma and leukemia, and many people report headaches if they consume it, even in small amounts. It is sold under the brand names NutraSweet and Equal, and is banned from organic foods for all these reasons, and more.

Other sugar substitutes are unrefined and natural, but have hidden drawbacks, either in terms of health problems, or because they don't work well in a home kitchen.

That's where this book can really help to guide you. It's a very good idea to avoid sugar, but I'll show you how to replace it in homemade desserts healthily, in a balanced way with practical home kitchens and a busy modern lifestyle in mind. I will help you change what you eat from a diet that probably contains too much sugar, to one that doesn't, but without adding lots of sugar replacements only to discover they're just as unhealthy as sugar, or even worse. And most importantly, I'll show you how to make them delicious!

Delicious makes the difference between owning a packet of 'healthy' sweetener, and actually eating it! Desserts are a part of life's great joys when eaten sensibly as a part of a healthy balanced diet that's rich in fresh fruit and vegetables.

Read on to discover the facts about many of the alternative sweeteners now becoming available, and to tempt your friends and family away from refined sugar-based puddings with delectable desserts made using the recipes in this book.

No-Sugar Sweeteners

RAW CANE SUGAR CRYSTALS

This is probably the most confusing ingredient to be listed as a sugar substitute, but it's not refined sugar. It's a valuable, minimally processed ingredient that surprisingly has many health benefits.

Raw cane sugar crystals are made from pure sugar cane juice that is evaporated. The crystals are high in minerals and because they are a complex, nutritionally rich food, they are low on the glycaemic index. Raw cane sugar crystals break down slowly, releasing sugars into the blood stream over a longer period of time, so it doesn't cause blood sugar spikes and crashes.

Sugar cane juice is a natural product found all over the world, wherever sugar cane is grown. It's made by pressing the cane through a rolling press, so it's an old-fashioned non-refined process that's also raw. The juice is then evaporated, either in the hot sun, or by being gently heated to preserve the nutrients. The residue that's left contains the phytonutrients in the plant, not just the sugars.

Refined sugar is made from either sugar cane or sugar beets. Raw cane sugar crystals come from the dried juice of a different variety of sugar cane than refined sugar, so despite the similarity in the name, it is a very different and far superior product, with an excellent mineral profile.

I totally recommend using it as a substitute for refined sugar, in moderation as always, and as a part of a balanced diet. It can be replaced in many recipes on a one-to-one basis for refined sugar and is very easy to use. It doesn't work in exactly the same way as refined sugar though, particularly when it comes to browning and caramelizing. I don't recommend using it in meringues and crème brulée but it is one of my favourite no-sugar ingredients because it's so full of minerals and helps maintain even blood sugar levels.

There's also a traditional Portuguese sugar called rapadura, which I recommended before raw sugar cane crystals became available. I still consider rapadura a good time-honoured natural product that could be used in moderation if you can't find the newer raw version. It's also made from raw sugar cane juice that's evaporated over a low heat, but unlike raw sugar cane crystals, it's not always made with the juice of an heirloom variety of the plant. Likewise, jaggery is a traditional sugar from India that's been enjoyed for millennia, but it's made by rapidly boiling the juice over a high heat which destroys many of the nutrients and enzymes in the juice. It's also not always made with heirloom cane varieties, so I don't recommend jaggery for this reason.

Beware of other sugar names that are just marketing jargon for refined sugar, such as evaporated cane sugar, evaporated cane juice, and of course, any of the familiar brown sugars, such as muscovado (molasses), turbinado and demerera (raw) . All of these products are just refined sugar with a bit of colour. They'll all create spikes and crashes in blood sugar, leach minerals and cause inflammatory responses in the short term and potentially in the long term as sugar-related diseases like diabetes and obesity.

Above: Raw cane sugar crystals

Raw cane sugar crystals are made from pure sugar cane juice that is evaporated. The crystals are high in minerals and it is low on the glycaemic index

Above: Stevia powder
Above right: Fresh dates

let's go no-no-sugar!

STEVIA – Stevia is a herb from Paraguay that's been enjoyed for centuries by the Guarani Indians. It's easy to grow in your garden and looks like mint or lemon balm, with green furry leaves. It has zero calories, which is the only natural sweetener to have this benefit.

If you pick a leaf off the plant and eat it, it tastes incredibly sweet, but it has a bitter aftertaste and strong herbal flavour that doesn't work well in every recipe. Fresh stevia can be used in fruit salads or cocktails, or blended into a pies or pudding. I like to think of it as a sweet, fresh leaf and use it as described. I'm happy to recommend it in this form.

Natural stevia leaves are available as a dried powder, which can be used like fresh stevia, but in smaller amounts as it becomes concentrated when it dries. Because of its flavour, it is tricky to use in its dried natural state. I sometimes add a pinch of dried stevia to smoothies if I'm using a strongly flavoured fruit as well, but in its dried form, it can be overpowering in flavour.

There are other processed stevia varieties available, including liquid stevia extract. These are best used in smoothies, nut and seed milks or to sweeten hot drinks. A little goes a long way. They are stevia leaves that have been soaked in alcohol to extract the active components in the herb, but without the bulk.

A white powdered extract of stevia is also available, which looks similar to refined white sugar. It does not have a herbal flavour because it is highly processed, so it is easier to use in baking. Although it has a natural base, this powdered, processed stevia cannot really be considered natural. It is about twice as sweet as refined sugar, and is processed to remove all of the sweet and bitter molecules inside the natural whole leaf except for rebaudioside A. The reb A powder is then usually bulked out with a neutral filler so it's the same sweetness as refined sugar to make it easy to replace cup for cup. Personally, I don't recommend this white stevia powder, as it's so highly processed that it bears no relation to the original herb.

DATES – Gone are the days when dates were only available in December, and were preserved in a sticky syrup made out of sugar! Instead, fresh dates are now available online and in stores, raw and unadulterated, and in different varieties that all have unique flavours and uses.

Dates come in three categories: soft, medium and dry. The soft ones are my favourite, including Medjool, Halawy, Barhi and Khadrawy. It's all about the texture, which is silky smooth and creamy, but also the flavours of these varieties are superior. Medium dates are also wonderful, although not quite as sweet. They are better in terms of storage, so they're a good choice to keep in the larder. It's easy to make them softer for use in recipes simply by soaking them in water for half an hour or so. Medium date varieties include Deglet Noor and Zahidi.

The dry ones aren't good to eat as they are, but can be soaked to make them more versatile. They're also known as 'bread dates' and include a variety called Thoory. I don't recommend these dates, simply because they're not very sweet, and they are not as versatile or delicious as the soft and medium dates.

There's a new product that's becoming available called date sugar. It's simply Thoory dates that have been fully desiccated and ground into a granular powder. Date sugar looks like dark brown sugar, but is about half as sweet. I love using fresh raw dates, and I recommend using them rather than date sugar if at all possible, as fresh dates are sweeter and taste better. However, I can recommend keeping a bag of date sugar in the back of your cupboard as an emergency sweetener because it's healthy and can be used in lots of recipes, including cookies, pies and smoothies. It's high in fibre and minerals, including copper, potassium and magnesium. It's also a good source of Vitamin B6, which is good for stress management.

Below, from left to right: Coconut crystals and coconut nectar

COCONUT CRYSTALS – This is a wonderful natural ingredient that is traditionally made in Thailand. It looks like brown sugar and has a subtle toffee flavour and good solubility. Before a coconut palm tree produces coconuts, the palm makes a large flower that is full of nectar. In traditional Thai culture, men climb these tall palm trees using a rope tied between their feet to aid their ascent. They cut the flowers along the base and leave a cup underneath the slit to collect the nectar. The nectar is brought down to earth, then gently cooked to evaporate the water.

This version of the product is available bottled as coconut nectar, but it is more usually available after it has been evaporated. As more water evaporates, it becomes a concentrated toffee that is then ground into crystals. Coconut crystals contain all the natural minerals of the original coconut flower nectar, but without the water content. It's rich in antioxidants, iron, zinc, calcium and potassium and is about three quarters as sweet as sugar.

Coconut crystals can be used in the same way as refined sugar. For this reason, dried coconut crystals are a versatile sugar substitute to have to hand. Coconut crystals are the same product as coconut sugar or coconut palm sugar. They are different names for the same thing. However, coconut palm sugar is a different thing from palm sugar, which is made by crushing the sap out of palm stems and evaporating the water from this juice.

I recommend using coconut crystals, but as with all sweet ingredients, it's best to eat it in moderation, not as a central part of the diet. I often bake with coconut crystals and have included it in many recipes so you can try it too.

I recommend only eating
honey in moderation,
even if it's the best quality,
as it is high on
the glycaemic index

**Below, clockwise from bottom left:
Crystallized honey, whipped honey,
clear honey and honeycomb**

HONEY – Clear, whipped and crystallized honeys are available, and all have subtly different uses in food preparation. As long as it's unpasteurized and raw, I am very happy to include it in my own diet, and to recommend it to you.

Clear honey can be the least-processed product if it's raw, but it's often only available pasteurized. As this is the most popular type, it's also the most likely to be from bees who have been fed a diet of sugar, which is the 'battery-farm' version of bee-keeping.

However, clear honey from organic farms that has not been pasteurized means that the honey was simply dripped out of the honeycomb and into the jar and sometimes is offered with a piece of the wax honeycomb inside the jar too. It is easy to use in recipes and is a healthy, natural food.

Whipped honey is the creamy version; opaque rather than transparent. It's lovely spread on toast or dissolved in tea, but is less often used in recipes. I like to add a drop of edible essential oil to a jar of whipped unpasteurized honey. Try stirring in a drop of lemon essential oil to make a simple lemon curd.

Honey that is unpasteurized becomes grainy and crystallized over time, whether its clear or whipped, and this texture can make it more useful for many recipes – including pastry, cakes and biscuits. The texture allows recipes to bind more easily, because it's stickier and also granular. It's almost worth keeping a jar of clear honey at the back of the cupboard specifically to allow it to crystallize. It's worth noting that some honeys are more resistant to crystallization than others, but the fastest ones include orange blossom, heather and avocado.

There's another form of honey that's more recently become available, which is a dried honey powder. It's usually processed with drying aids and bulking agents, and sometimes even contains added artifical sweeteners, so it's best avoided. Like table salt, dried honey powder contains anti-caking agents to ensure it is free-flowing. It doesn't have any place in my own kitchen.

I love eating unpasteurized honey in small amounts, and think of it as a medicinal food rather than a sweetener. I recommend only eating raw honey for this reason, as the heat used to pasteurize honey destroys most of the medicinal benefits.

That said, I definitely recommend only eating honey in moderation as it is high on the glycaemic index. If you're diabetic or pre-diabetic, it's best to avoid it altogether, or to stick to bee pollen or royal jelly in small amounts.

The healing benefits contained in all bee products are a part of the richness of this special wholefood. I believe that honey is a beneficial part of a balanced diet when eaten in sensible amounts, as it always has been around the

world, in almost every culture. Explore the many varieties now available, including manuka, buckwheat, and the single herbal and floral varieties.

Avoid eating refined, pasteurized honey, as it's simply sugar without most of the original nutrients. Raw, unpasteurized honey boosts immunity and supports the respiratory system when fighting flu or resisting common pollen allergies.

AGAVE NECTAR – This is one of the most confusing and controversial no-sugar ingredients at the moment, with conflicting advice and misinformation freely given on the internet and by health professionals. Personally, I recommend real raw agave nectar without any reservations, and I hate agave that isn't real and isn't raw, because it's a completely different product. The truth is that real agave is not bad for you, but it all depends on the brand because most brands aren't real agave. More often than not, they are high-fructose corn syrup that's labelled agave. This is why most syrup sold as agave tastes awful, and looks like thin, high-fructose corn syrup. It is nothing like the natural gel that comes from the agave plant. However, good-quality agave syrup is a wonderful ingredient that looks and tastes very different from the products found in most high street stores. It's minimally processed, tastes beautiful and is thick and almost gelatinous with a texture comparable to aloe vera gel. It has a very steady effect on blood sugar and also acts as a prebiotic, meaning it's good for your internal flora. It's a healthy sweetener and I recommend it as a sugar-replacement, especially for use in raw recipes.

I recommend using a brand called Ultimate Superfoods and their sub-brand Ojio, which is available in the UK and USA. There's also a fantastic blue agave nectar available in in the USA, which is grown in Texas at Glaser Organic Farm.

Agave nectar and agave syrup are the same product – it's just a different name for the same thing. Agave is also available in powdered form and can be used in some recipes as an icing (confectioners') sugar substitute. However, it does not act exactly the same as icing (confectioners') sugar. It isn't stable because it is highly absorbent and is only half as sweet.

Ultimate Superfoods offer powdered agave under their Ojio brand and I don't recommend it for general use, but do like to sprinkle it on to baked goods just before serving, as it looks similar to icing (confectioners') sugar while it remains dry. After about an hour, it loses the white colour and becomes a transparent sticky coating.

ASPARTAME – this artificial sweetener is widely acknowledged to have an effect on the brain's ability to detect when the body has eaten enough, and so it has the opposite effect on dieting than intended. Although it is low-calorie, it encourages the body to continue to crave food after it has been ingested, so it assists obesity. Highly processed, with zero beneficial nutrients, this sweetener is best avoided at all costs! It's been linked to numerous cancers, particularly blood cancers, and is often cited as causing headaches, dizziness and nausea.

MAPLE SYRUP – I enjoy using maple syrup because although it isn't very low on the glycaemic index, it has such a delicious flavour – especially if it's a high-quality, small-batch maple syrup. Even though its effect on blood sugar is as powerful as refined sugar, it still has a place in my larder because it's something that I regard more as a flavouring than a no-sugar sweetener. It should just be eaten in moderation, which is easy becuase a little goes a long way!

This delicious sweetener has a history that's as unique as its flavour. Invented by the Quakers in the United States, maple syrup was the result of their conscientious objection to the American cane sugar industry, which was the main reason for the slave trade in the southern states. Quaker woodsmen discovered that the maple trees growing on the east coast could be tapped for their sap

Above: Agave nectar

Above: Maple syrup and maple sugar

I enjoy using maple syrup because although it isn't very low on the glycaemic index, it has such a wonderful flavour — especially if it's a high-quality, small-batch maple syrup. It has a place in my larder because it's something that I regard more as a flavouring than a no-sugar sweetener

in the spring months without harming the trees. The sap is collected and boiled in huge vats over extremely hot wood fires out in the forest for up to a week, until the natural sap has been concentrated to about forty times its original water content. The whole process of tapping the trees, collecting the sap and boiling it into syrup is a community activity, with people needed to stay awake throughout the night to tend to the fires, so a tradition of folk music and song has sprung up around these maple vigils. This traditional maple culture still very much survives today, with families and friends getting together for the boiling week, and music and merriment all day and all night in the forests while the fires burn.

There's a more industrialized maple syrup industry as well, of course, but it's impossible to cut many of the corners when making maple syrup. The most commercial operations do tap the trees for greater sap production, and local heirloom maple syrup producers are often critical of their sapping techniques in terms of the health and longevity of the trees. However, in terms of the product, more commercial maple syrup is made in a very similar way from the sap. It's simply concentrated in big vats inside a factory, not in the forest.

Maple syrup is available in many different grades, as well as in levels of amber, from light to dark. There is a big range and connoisseurs prefer to seek out maple syrup made in small batches. All maple syrup varieties contain iron, calcium and zinc. Beware of the false 'maple syrup flavour' products that are just high-fructose corn syrup with artificial flavourings added. Always read the label to make sure you're buying 100% real maple syrup, whichever the grade or colour. Maple syrup is also available as maple sugar, which is the same product but concentrated still further until it's granulated. Maple sugar has the delicious buttery flavour of the syrup and can be used as a direct sugar replacement for refined sugar in many recipes, because it has a similar sweetness.

POLYOLS – This group of low-calorie sugar substitutes includes xylitol, erythritol, sorbitol, malitol, lactitol and isomalt. It is a group of highly processed sweeteners that are manufactured from plant alcohols made from fermented hardwood. Once exclusively sold to commercial food manufacturers, they have recently started to become available to domestic kitchens as powders, or in granulated form.

They are easy to use in baking and are found in many processed foods because of their low calories. They do have a strange cooling effect on the tongue that is hard to describe, so this detracts from their subtlety in baked goods, but it can be countered by using a liquid polyol known as vegetable glycerin, described on the next page, or by adding hot spices like ground ginger.

Polyols have an extremely low glycaemic index and are difficult for the body to digest, so they pass through the digestive tract almost unaltered, in a similar way to roughage. There is some speculation that they may have a similar beneficial effect on the digestive flora that insoluble fibre has, providing a good habitat for probiotic cultures to thrive. However, there is also speculation that it may be a toxic environment for internal flora, or that it may distort the relative amounts of different floral colonies in a way that may be unsafe in the long term. We don't know yet because these ingredients haven't been used for a long enough period of time to truly know what they do for internal flora.

Whether it is good or bad for probiotic health, this group of sweeteners is highly processed and relatively new to human consumption, so I suggest they should be regarded as novel and untested. They are fantastic in terms of calories, many of them having zero calories and a negligible effect on blood sugar levels, so are perfect for diabetics wanting a birthday cake. However, at present, I would only recommend using polyols now and then for specific occasions, rather than for everyday use. I rely on foods that have been tested on multiple previous generations to form the core of my diet and am wary of ingredients that are developed outside of human evolution, in a laboratory environment, without many peer-evaluated studies. I've included a recipe using xylitol because it seemed like a good balance, as I wouldn't want to entirely negate their place in a no-sugar diet. I'm excited to be able to bake birthday cakes for people with diabetes, but you won't find me going back for a second slice...

GLYCERIN – Like all polyols, glycerin, or glycerol as it's also known, has a very low glycaemic index, so it's useful for people who have diabetes. Unlike the powdered polyols described above, glycerin is a clear, viscous liquid that's high in calories, but is deeply moistening when used in recipes.

Glycerin is about half as sweet as refined sugar, but has roughly the same amount of calories per teaspoon so it makes no sense as part of a calorie-controlled diet. However, it does have a much lower glycaemic index, meaning that despite having a lot of calories, it won't make your blood sugar spike and crash. Like all polyols, it has a strange effect on bacteria in the intestines and is a mild laxative.

Although it's possible to make glycerin from vegetable or animal fat, almost all commercially available glycerin is a bi-product of the biodiesel industry, so it's a highly processed ingredient. It's mostly useful for its moistening qualities, which can make a marzipan on a cake that's flexible instead of hard, or to add to a cake to make sure it's more succulent and delectable.

I'm not actively against it, but it's not something I recommend eating more regularly than perhaps once or twice a year in the marzipan around your Yule Log, or inside a wedding cake that you'd like to be particularly moist.

AMAZAKE – this Japanese porridge is made by fermenting grains, but instead of refining them like a malt syrup, the grains are kept. It's a good ingredient to experiment with as an addition to puddings and smoothies. It's also great eaten on its own straight from the jar. It's not useful as an ingredient in baked goods, as it's more like yogurt. I recommend it, as it's a living fermented food full of flora.

MONK FRUIT EXTRACT – While monk fruit is a natural healthy fruit that is sweet and could theoretically be a useful ingredient, it is most widely available as monk fruit extract mixed into a powdered product that is about 90% dextrose. Unless you are certain that the product you are buying is 100% dried monk fruit, it's best to avoid products that contain monk fruit extract for this reason. Always read the label, as the ingredients legally have to state whether the product contains anything other than monk fruit. At the time of writing, there are no monk fruit products available anywhere in the world that purely contain monk fruit. All of them are mostly dextrose and are best avoided for this reason.

Above: Amazake

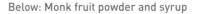

Below: Monk fruit powder and syrup

SUCRALOSE – This is another artificial sweetener that I do not ever eat myself or recommend, even for occasional use. It's possibly even worse for human health than aspartame and has no place in a no-sugar diet.

It's made by chlorinating refined sugar, which means they add chlorine to refined sugar in a laboratory setting, in order to further process refined sugar. Sucralose is high on the glycaemic index and causes obesity and diabetes, as well as being closely linked to leukemia in peer-reviewed medical studies. It also reduces the beneficial flora that are essential for digestive health.

Above, left to right: Licorice sticks, licorice powder and vanilla pods (beans)
Above right: Yacon syrup

DEXTROSE/MALTODEXTRIN – Dextrose is another word for glucose. It is exactly the same thing and is a highly-processed ingredient with a very high glycaemic index. Maltodextrin is a slightly more complex sugar, but is broken down quickly into the blood stream, resulting in sugar spikes. Avoid them, because they are even more processed than refined sugar and cause just as much damage, if not more.

SPICES – While not technically sweet, some spices can be used to accentuate the sweetness of other ingredients. Cinnamon adds sweetness to dishes while supporting the body's insulin production. Licorice can be used as a powder, or as a tea made from steeped licorice sticks. Use licorice or cinnamon teas in recipes that require liquids to be added, and add to smoothies. I also recommend using vanilla, as it is a wonderful sweetener for many recipes.

Below, clockwise from bottom left:
Coconut, mesquite and chestnut flours

YACON – Yacon is a tuber from South America and can be used in its fresh state, but it is most widely available as yacon syrup. In either form, yacon acts as a prebiotic in the digestive system in a similar way to oats, so it's good for internal health as well as being a versatile sweetener. I recommend using yacon syrup to replace corn syrup or maple syrup for a lower glycaemic rating, and it's good to try it in powder form for baking. It's not overly sweet, which is a bonus. If used as a replacement for corn syrup one-on-one, the finished baked goods will be about half as sweet, which is often a perfect conversion for my own tastebuds.

Yacon powder is something I use more as a sweet flour to bake cookies, or to add to smoothies as a thickener. I find it's best to use it in moderation, as the prebiotic effect can be a little more vigorous than intended for polite company.

SWEET FLOURS – Sometimes it's good to replace some of the flour in a recipe with non-wheat flours that are naturally sweet. These include mesquite flour, chestnut flour and coconut flour. They add subtle sweetness and flavour to recipes and they are also universally gluten-free. Use them wisely, as they don't act the same way as wheat flour in baked goods. Start trying them by replacing about a quarter of the amount of wheat flour with one of these gluten-free sweet flours, except for any recipe involving yeast. For yeast-based baking, it's best to avoid them, but for cakes, try them all as a part of a flour mixture.

SWEET OILS – Some oils are subtly sweet due to being extracted from nuts and seeds, but some are more markedly sweet than others. Choose coconut oil for sweet recipes, for example, for shallow frying pancakes or fritters. Also hazelnut oil is naturally sweeter than most true nut oils and pistachio oil is a wonderful choice. I recommend investing in a collection of sweet oils, and keeping them refrigerated to avoid them going rancid.

FRUIT POWDERS – Freeze-dried fruit powders are starting to become available and they are a lot of fun! That said, some of them are not very sweet, because many berries are tart in their fresh state. I recommend you try them, and you'll discover how their flavours can sometimes fool the taste buds into believing a dessert is sweeter than it is, in the same way that vanilla can.

Dried strawberry powder is a fabulous ingredient to dust on fruit salads, as is mango powder. It's also useful in any dishes with a Thai or Indian feeling, adding a little piquancy. Try sprinkling dried pomegranate powder on to anything at all as a garnish. It creates a dark and incredible colour contrast, and is fabulous as a natural food colouring for anything raw or lightly cooked, like a custard pudding.

Dried banana powder is a very sweet fruit powder and is fun to use in custards, shakes and baked goods. It's the sweetest of the dried fruit powders, and so it's perhaps the most versatile. See my recipe for Banana Creamsicles for a yummy example of how it can be enjoyed.

There are freeze-dried fruit powders now available for fruits that aren't available commercially in their fresh form. While it's totally possible to grow yumberry trees in many Western climates, fresh yumberries aren't available outside of Asia. As their name suggests, they're yummy! Yumberry powder is red and very rich in antioxidants. It's a fun and useful powder to track down, although sadly the bright red colour doesn't hold up when baked.

Another fruit that's unavailable in fresh form, but that's found as dried powder, is lucuma. Widely available and very popular in Peru, lucuma fruit have a mild and smooth flavour not unlike creamy, fruity vanilla. The powder is fabulous to mix into smoothies and raw cream pies, as well as ice cream for a classic spin.

Baobab fruit grow in dry regions of Madagascar, Africa and Australia, on some of the oldest trees on earth. Baobab trees are known as the tree of life as they have fruit and hold water in their trunks, as well as being a source of fibre for textiles and providing firewood. The dried fruit powder is a pale colour, and has a creamy flavour with a hint of sherbet. The fruit are rich in vitamin C and other antioxidants, so it's best to use baobab powder in raw dishes or as a raw dusting powder for cooked desserts, so that heat doesn't destroy these nutrients.

As with fresh fruit, the sweetness in fruit powders comes from natural fruit sugars, so they should be eaten in small amounts. These powders have intense flavours along with their sweetness, so you'll have no problem keeping their use to sensible amounts in terms of the sugars they naturally contain.

I thoroughly recommend exploring fruit powders because of the incredible concentrated amounts of phytonutrients they contain, including cancer-fighting antioxidants of every kind, as well as their wonderful flavours and colours.

DRIED FRUITS – Dried fruits are widely used in traditional recipes that contain sugar, but if you raise the amount of dried fruit, you can often lower the amount of refined sugars. Of course, the sweetness of the dried fruit is chemically not unlike the sweetness of the refined sugar, but as a part of a whole food, it is released more slowly into the blood stream, and is accompanied by the vitamins, minerals, enzymes and phytonutrients that are in the fruit that it's made from.

I recommend trying the following dried fruits: raisins, sultanas (golden raisins), currants, dates, figs, blueberries, mulberries, plums, cherries, mango, cantaloupe, papaya and apricots.

Above, clockwise from bottom: Coconut, hazelnut and pistachio oils

Below: Banana and strawberry powders; dried strawberries

Above, clockwise from top: Dried apricots, figs, cherries, mulberries, apple and pineapple

Below, clockwise from bottom left: Apple and blueberry, pear and apple and pear fruit purées

Although all kinds of dried fruit contain sugars, different varieties contain different amounts of nutrients, and the way they are dried hugely affects their nutritional content. I usually choose the dried fruit I eat based on the amount of phytonutrients it contains, as much as the flavour profile. I also choose on the basis of whether they've been sun-dried or freeze-dried. For example, currants contain high quantities of antioxidants, much higher than sultanas (golden raisins) or raisins, so I tend to use Zante currants more than sultanas. If I do use sultanas, it's generally varieties made from red grapes, not white grapes, as the red ones contain more antioxidants.

Many nutrients are damaged by exposure to heat and light, so sun-dried currants contain lower levels of phytonutrients than freeze-dried currants. The same is true for most varieties of dried fruit, so freeze-dried fruit is preferable.

Always read the ingredients label when buying dried fruit, as some varieties routinely contain sugar. For example, most dried blueberries are soaked in sugar syrup and oil before being packed, but it's possible to find freeze-dried blueberries that are sugar-free and I recommend them for use in baked goods, as well as for snacking. They act differently when baked into a cake, but I prefer them. They feel more like a real fruit in the finished product and less like a fancy raisin.

Dried plums are the same as prunes and are a wonderful sweetener. It's possible to find dried whole Alpine strawberries that have been soaked in apple juice, which makes them moist and soft, with a consistency similar to apple rings and an intense strawberry flavour. Luscious!

HIGH FRUCTOSE CORN SYRUP – This is one of my least favourite sweeteners, and for good reason. It is devoid of any vitamins, minerals or phytonutrients and is high in calories. It also has one of the highest glycaemic indexes of almost any ingredient. In spite of this it is eaten every day, as one of the most ubiquitous sweeteners in the world. It causes obesity and diabetes and it leaches minerals from bones. It causes soft tissues to become inflamed, causes headaches, and it can cause nausea. No thanks!

FRUIT SYRUPS AND FRUIT CONCENTRATES – Northern European cuisines include a range of fruit concentrates, and are particularly fond of apple and pear syrups and molasses. They're found in Scandinavian kitchens and from Denmark to France. Use them like honey, either spread on toast or dissolved and mixed into a recipe. In the USA, apple concentrate is sold under the name bee-free honey. Mediterranean cuisines also include fruit concentrates, but more often call for more complex flavours like pomegranate molasses, which are less sweet but still have their place in a healthy low-sugar diet. As with fruit powders and dried fruits, I recommend syrups and concentrates, but only in small amounts.

Fruit purées and fruit butters are good to have on hand, or to keep in the freezer. Try adding apple sauce made from cooking down fresh apples, or pear sauce made in the same way. Stoned (pitted) fruit are wonderful preserved simply as a purée and berries can be frozen and used without any need for cooking at all.

MALT SYRUPS – For centuries, grains have been fermented to produce malt syrups that are low in simple sugars that are slowly released into the bloodstream. I recommend using brown rice malt syrup and barley malt syrup. Try drizzling on to pancakes as a substitute for maple syrup, or using them in baked goods.

They are not as sweet as other ingredients, for example honey, and they have a lingering aftertaste that works well in some recipes, but is sometimes distracting from the central flavours. I recommend experimenting with traditional malt syrups and enjoying them in sensible quantities as a part of a balanced diet.

Bear in mind that malt syrups are basically grains that have been partially pre-digested by enzymes in a fermentation process. As such, they have a higher glycaemic index than the original whole grains they are generated from, but still have a lower glycaemic index than processed sugar syrups. Barley malt syrup has a gentler effect on the blood stream than brown rice malt syrup, so I recommend barley malt syrup over brown rice malt syrup.

TAPIOCA SYRUP – made from the starch of cassava tubers, tapioca syrup is a new ingredient that's recently been developed by an American manufacturer, Ciranda. They have developed a wide selection of tapioca syrups for different uses, for example, one that is more binding, one that is sweeter, and another that is less sticky and therefore better for making hard sweets or candies.

All tapioca syrups are made by fermenting cassava tuber starch, and all have an initial quick release of sugars into the blood stream, and then a longer release afterwards as the complex carbohydrates are slowly broken down. As these syrups are processed and have a quick release aspect to their sugars, I don't recommend using them much, but a little can be helpful as a binder or a glaze.

BLACK TREACLE OR BLACKSTRAP MOLASSES – this is where the goodness goes when it's removed from sugar in the refining process. Blackstrap molasses is full of beneficial minerals including iron, copper, manganese, potassium and magnesium. It has an alkalinizing effect on the body, and so it works as a gentle anti inflammatory.

Vegetarians often eat molasses as a source of iron, but it's important to eat organic molasses, as the sugar cane industry is heavily reliant on pesticides. As a result, pesticides are found in high concentrations in molasses that isn't organic. I recommend molasses in baked goods where its strong flavour will be enjoyed. It's not a subtle ingredient, but used as the primary flavouring, molasses makes perfect cookies and is delicious in hot drinks.

MIRACLE BERRIES – These little berries are around the size of a large goji berry or a small olive and have a big pit relative to the size of their flesh, like olives. They are from a shrub from Ghana that can be grown as a houseplant in temperate climates and are unlike any other berry.

Miracle berries work by temporarily switching off the sour receptors in your mouth so that only the sweet receptors can be experienced. To try them, chew the fresh berry and swish it around the mouth so that every internal surface is coated. Try eating a raw lemon immediately afterwards, and it will taste like the sweetest lemon sherbet you've ever experienced. Try eating anything at all for the next 15 minutes and it will taste incredibly sweet and delicious, after which the effect fades, the sour taste receptors reopen and everything goes back to normal.

While there are obvious dangers in overdoing this, like binging on everything because it taste so amazing, when approached sensibly, these little berries are a lot of fun and could be used to eliminate the need to add any kind of sweetener to a final course at a dinner party. They're social, fun and can be fantastic when tried with a group of friends at a dinner party.

The berries are available frozen or in granulated form, and also as a powder that has been formed into tablets.

Above, clockwise from top left: Lavender and pomegranate syrups; pear and apple spread

Below, left to right: Blackstrap molasses and malt syrup

Hot Puddings, Crumbles and Custard

On a cold night, there is nothing more comforting than a warming dessert to enjoy by the fire. Winter's delight is a hot crumble served with lashings of creamy custard, but this doesn't mean it has to be packed with sugar. There are less traditional, simpler and quicker ways to produce these hearty dishes. Whether it's a caramelized pineapple sponge, a sweet berry taco, or a rich chocolate custard, these no-sugar desserts are guaranteed to deliver pure coziness with every spoonful.

Hot puddings on a cold night are the definition of comfort, as you enjoy every warm and tempting spoonful

This warming crumble is cooked to perfection by baking in two stages. The apple layer is baked first so that it cooks thoroughly without the crumble topping burning or drying. The crumble is then baked again to make the topping deliciously crunchy and crisp.

The honey and maple syrup in this recipe enhance the natural caramelization of the apples, which is useful if using a variety that is less sweet. However, the honey can be reduced if you are using apples that are naturally sweeter. If you're using traditional cooking apples that are more tart, add extra honey and maple syrup to taste. Serve with cream, coconut cream, or with an old movie for perfect nostalgia.

Perfect Apple Crumble

SERVES 12

15ml/1 tbsp vegetable oil, for greasing
50g/2oz/½ cup ground almonds
90g/3½oz/¾ cup wholemeal (whole-wheat) flour
90g/3½oz/1 cup rolled oats
5ml/1 tsp ground cinnamon
175g/6oz/¾ cup cold coconut oil or unsalted butter, diced
30ml/2 tbsp honey, plus 30ml/2 tbsp extra, to sweeten (optional)
30ml/2 tbsp maple syrup, plus 30ml/ 2 tbsp extra, to sweeten (optional)
120ml/4fl oz/½ cup apple juice
1.5ml/¼ tsp ground ginger
a pinch of ground nutmeg
6–8 medium apples

1 Preheat the oven to 180°C/350°F/ Gas 4. Lightly grease a 23cm x 23cm/9in x 9in shallow baking dish with oil.

2 Put the ground almonds, flour, oats and 2.5ml/½ tsp of the cinnamon in a bowl and mix to combine.

3 Add the coconut oil or butter and quickly rub it into the almond and oat mixture, allowing visible pea-sized pieces to remain.

4 Warm the honey by immersing the sealed jar in a bowl of hot water. When liquid, mix 30ml/2 tbsp of the honey with the maple syrup and apple juice in a small bowl.

5 Sprinkle a tablespoon of the liquid around the almond and oat mixture, and fluff with a fork. Put it in the refrigerator to chill.

6 Stir the spices into the apple juice mixture. Core and quarter the apples and put them in the prepared baking dish. Pour the apple juice mixture over

the top and drizzle over the additional honey and maple syrup, if using.

7 Cover with foil and bake for 45 minutes–1 hour, then remove the foil and test the apples. The time different varieties of apples take to bake varies greatly, so use a fork to check how soft they are. If they seem almost cooked, sprinkle the chilled crumble mixture evenly over the top.

8 Raise the oven temperature to 220°C/425°F/Gas 7. Return the baking dish to the oven, uncovered, and bake for 20–30 minutes more, or until the topping is golden brown. Remove the crumble from the oven and allow to stand for about 10 minutes before serving.

If you're a fan of your grandma's old-fashioned pineapple upside-down cake, this will be your new favourite recipe. Using fresh pineapple instead of canned, these steamed desserts make the most of the natural sweetness of the fruit, which is caramelized before it is added to the batter. They are perfect served warm with coconut cream or sugar-free ice cream.

Caramelized Pineapple Desserts

SERVES 6

15g/½oz sugar-free dried pineapple, shredded
30ml/2 tbsp cold coconut oil
1 fresh pineapple
115g/4oz/½ cup unsalted butter, plus 15ml/1 tbsp, for greasing
60ml/4 tbsp maple syrup
150g/5oz/1 cup coconut crystals
4 eggs
150g/5oz/1¼ cups plain (all-purpose) flour, plus 15ml/1 tbsp for dusting
10ml/2 tsp baking powder
2.5ml/½ tsp nutmeg
grated rind of 1 lemon

1 Grease six ceramic ramekins with butter and lightly dust them with flour.

2 Put the dried, shredded pineapple and coconut oil in a bowl. Mix to combine and set aside to soak.

3 Bring a double boiler, or large pan, of water to the boil to steam the desserts.

4 Peel and core the fresh pineapple, then cut into 2.5cm/1in square chunks.

5 Melt 15ml/1 tbsp of the butter in a frying pan over a high heat. Add the maple syrup and fresh pineapple and fry, stirring constantly, until the syrup has reduced and the fruit has caramelized to a golden brown. Put an equal amount of pineapple and syrup into each of the prepared ramekins and set aside.

6 Cream the remaining butter and coconut crystals in a mixing bowl using an electric whisk on medium for about 2 minutes. Beat in the eggs one by one.

7 Sift in the flour, baking powder and nutmeg, and fold into the batter using a silicone spatula. Fold in the soaked, dried shredded pineapple and oil mixture, and the lemon rind.

8 Spoon the batter equally into the ramekins and cover with baking parchment tightly enough to seal in the moisture, but loosely enough that the desserts are able to rise above the rim of the ramekins. Tie with string.

9 Put the desserts in the top of the double boiler, or in a steamer set inside a large pan of boiling water. Steam the desserts for about 40 minutes, topping up with extra boiling water, if needed.

10 Remove the desserts from the pan and allow to cool in the ramekins for about 10 minutes. Turn them out on to individual serving plates and serve.

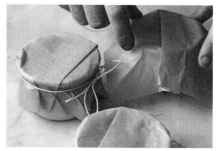

Sweet potatoes come in many varieties and are often sold with information about their relative sweetness, especially if you buy them at a farmers' market. All varieties work wonderfully in this recipe.

For a lighter option, feel free to substitute the ground almonds with wholemeal (whole-wheat) flour or gluten-free flours such as rice flour, fine corn meal or potato flour. Simply replace the ground almonds with the same amount of your chosen flour. Serve with a generous dollop of yogurt, coconut cream or stewed apples and sprinkled with cinnamon.

Sweet Potato Cakes

SERVES 4

15ml/1 tbsp vegetable oil, for greasing
500g/1¼lb sweet potatoes
45ml/3 tbsp ground almonds
2.5ml/½ tsp ground cinnamon, plus
  extra for sprinkling
1.5ml/¼ tsp ground nutmeg
0.6ml/⅛ tsp baking powder
2 eggs, lightly beaten
Greek (US strained plain) yogurt,
  to serve (optional)

1 Preheat the oven to 220°C/425°F/ Gas 7. Grease a baking sheet with oil and line it with baking parchment.

2 Grate the unpeeled sweet potatoes using a food processor or a box grater, then spread them out on a clean dish towel to absorb any excess juices.

3 Put the grated sweet potatoes in a mixing bowl with the ground almonds, spices and baking powder. Add the eggs and mix to combine, working quickly.

4 Divide the mixture into eight equal portions and put them on the baking sheet. Flatten each portion so they are round, and about 1cm/½in thick.

5 Bake for 15 minutes on one side, then remove from the oven briefly. Flip each of the cakes over and rotate the baking sheet before returning it to the oven. Bake for 10 minutes more, or until the cakes are crispy and brown.

6 Serve two hot cakes per person, with a spoonful of Greek yogurt and sprinkled with cinnamon.

Feel free to substitute the ground almonds with wholemeal flour or gluten-free flours such as rice flour, fine corn meal or potato flour

Tacos are the ultimate Mexican finger food, but to my knowledge, they're never served with a sweet filling, and are usually pretty meaty. Here they are served as a sweet vegan treat, still eaten hot but made with fresh, seasonal fruit, or with frozen berries after the summer has passed. Either way, this dessert will be sticky, messy and delicious! Try it with hard taco shells or soft taco shells to suit your taste, but try to find organic tacos if you can, as non-organic corn is usually tainted with GMOs.

Sweet Tacos

SERVES 4

350g/12oz firm tofu, drained and sliced
juice and grated rind of 1 lime
30ml/2 tbsp coconut oil
60ml/4 tbsp maple syrup
8 fresh or frozen strawberries, hulled
8 small corn taco shells

1 Arrange the tofu slices in a shallow dish. Pour over the lime juice and rind and set aside to marinate for half an hour.

2 When you're ready to prepare the tacos, heat the oil in a small pan over a medium heat. Add the marinated tofu, lime, maple syrup and the strawberries and cook, stirring regularly, until soft and piping hot.

3 Heat the tortillas one by one in a dry frying pan for about 30 seconds on each side until hot. Keep hot by putting them inside a clean dish towel when each one is ready.

4 Assemble the tacos by stacking two tortillas on each serving plate, then spooning an equal amount of the tofu and strawberry mixture on to each. Pour any remaining syrup from the pan over the warm tacos. Serve immediately.

This is probably the quickest recipe to prepare in the book. Almost instant, it's a hot dessert that makes a crowd-pleasing end to any week-day dinner. Children love it as much as adults and it can be served in countless ways by adding different toppings, sauces and spices. It's sweet, warming and comforting.

Fried Bananas

SERVES 4
30ml/2 tbsp coconut oil
30ml/2 tbsp honey
10ml/2 tsp ground cinnamon
4 ripe bananas, sliced lengthways
coconut cream, to serve (optional)

1 Heat the oil, honey and cinnamon in a large frying pan over a medium heat.

2 Add the bananas and cook for 1–2 minutes on one side. Turn them over carefully and cook the other side for 1–2 minutes more.

3 Serve drizzled with coconut cream, if liked, and eat immediately.

COOK'S TIP
Coconut cream is the thick part of coconut milk that rises to the top. It can be used as a substitute for dairy cream. It has roughly the same fat content as whipping cream.

This is an indulgent recipe because the apples are deep fried, but no sugar is used as they are naturally sweetened with a coconut batter. Use very fresh apples, or they will turn into mush while they fry. Crisp, firm apples stay together and cook into meltingly soft and delicious rings.

I've recommended apple cider for this recipe, but feel free to use a no-sugar carbonated drink instead, such as mineral water or strong apple cider. Make sure that the liquid is ice-cold because this makes a huge difference to how the batter will puff up when dropped into the hot oil.

Tempura Apples

SERVES 4

4 medium or 6 small apples
750ml/1¼ pints/3 cups high-heat
  sunflower, safflower or groundnut
  (peanut) oil, for frying
125g/4¼oz/generous 1 cup coconut
  flour, plus extra for dusting
60g/2¼oz/½ cup cornflour (cornstarch)
5ml/1 tsp ground cinnamon
2 eggs, beaten
350ml/12fl oz/1½ cups ice-cold dry
  (hard) apple cider
creamy goat's cheese, maple syrup and
  cinnamon, to serve (optional)

1 Core the apples and slice into 5mm/¼in rings. Lay them on a clean dish towel and put another clean dish towel on top to remove any juice from the surface.

2 Heat the oil in a large pan over a high heat, or in an electric fryer.

3 Sift the coconut flour, cornflour and cinnamon into a large mixing bowl. Add the eggs and cider and stir to combine. It's fine if there are lumps.

4 Drop a spoonful of the batter into the oil to test whether it is hot enough. When it is ready, the batter becomes golden brown in about 20 seconds.

5 When the oil is hot, dredge the apple slices in the batter and drop them into the pan in batches of three. Turn them as they cook using a slotted spoon.

6 Remove each batch of apple rings when they are golden brown and leave to drain on a wire rack set over a baking sheet (with sides). Keep frying and draining until all of the apple rings have been cooked.

7 Serve on their own, or with creamy goat's cheese drizzled with maple syrup and sprinkled with cinnamon, if liked.

Imagine the warmth of baked apples, but with the kind of crispy exterior that can only be achieved by deep-frying

A true egg custard is wonderful, but I recommend you try this vegan custard recipe, even if you're not vegan. It's so simple and quick to prepare, and has the nostalgia of childhood wrapped into its silky smooth texture and chocolatey taste. It can be served as a pudding on its own, or as an indulgent chocolate topping for other desserts.

With this almond milk recipe, you'll be delighted, whatever your dietary preference. What could go better together than chocolate and almonds?

Vegan Chocolate Custards

SERVES 4
75ml/5 tbsp raw cacao powder
60ml/4 tbsp cornflour (cornstarch)
60ml/4 tbsp agave nectar
250ml/½ pint/2 cups unsweetened
  almond milk
125ml/8fl oz/½ cup water
5ml/1 tsp vanilla extract (optional)

1 Sift the dry ingredients into a medium pan and slowly add the almond milk and water, whisking continuously as you do so. Alternatively, put all of the ingredients in a high-speed blender and blend on the high setting for about 1 minute.

2 Heat the mixture over a low–medium heat, whisking constantly, to avoid lumps. Add the vanilla, if using.

3 Slowly bring to the boil and cook for about 1 minute, still whisking.

4 Set the custard aside in the pan for about 10 minutes to thicken, then serve, either in four individual serving glasses as a dessert, or poured over a dessert of your choice as a topping.

Try any kind of milk, including dairy milk if you're not vegan

ALMOND MILK
I never buy almond milk in a carton because it's so quick and easy to make at home. It tastes a hundred times better, is about a quarter of the price and it doesn't contain any of the additives that are in the store-bought variety. You'll need double this amount of almond milk to make this custard.

60ml/4 tbsp raw almonds, soaked in
  water overnight and drained
250ml/8fl oz/1 cup water
15ml/1 tbsp raw agave syrup
1–2 drops vanilla extract (optional)

Put the almonds, water and agave syrup in a blender and blend on high until smooth. Strain through a piece of muslin or cheesecloth into a large bowl and stir in the vanilla, if liked.

Jellies, Mousses and Soufflés

My childhood memories are strewn with jellies, brightly coloured and without doubt full of the kind of artificial chemistry that littered the 1970s. Today's jellies wobble just as much, yet deliver their wibble without any quibble. Whether vegan or gelatine-based, these no-sugar mousses, soufflés and jellies are as elegant and grown-up as you, but many can be served to the pint-sized people in your life as well. Whether a soufflé or a zabaglione, they're as light and delightful on your tongue as they are angelic on your waistline.

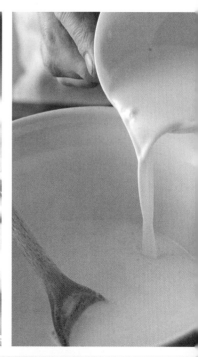

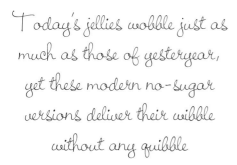

Today's jellies wobble just as much as those of yesteryear, yet these modern no-sugar versions deliver their wibble without any quibble

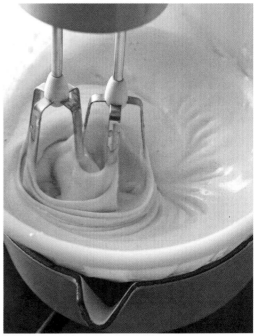

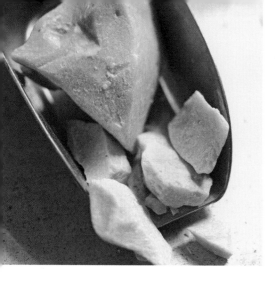

Cacao butter is available at good health food stores and online. Packed with heart-healthy fats and oils, it adds a delicious depth of flavour and smooth texture to all kinds of recipes, including these chic parfaits.

Lucuma powder is a nutritiously-dense fruit that's full of betacarotene and B vitamins, and it has a creamy subtle flavour that's related to maple syrup.

Start preparing this the day before serving, as the cashews and almonds must be soaked for at least 4 hours or overnight in separate bowls, to soften. Definitely more of an adult dessert than one for the children, it is best enjoyed after dinner with an espresso.

White Chocolate and Strawberry Parfaits

SERVES 6
115g/4oz/½ cup cacao butter
50g/2oz/½ cup cashew pieces, soaked in the refrigerator for at least 4 hours, or overnight
2 ripe avocados
350g/12oz/3 cups strawberries, hulled
120ml/4 fl oz/½ cup maple syrup
juice of ½ lemon
5ml/1 tsp ground vanilla pods (beans)
115g/4oz/1 cup almonds, soaked in the refrigerator for at least 4 hours, or overnight
90g/3½oz/1 cup rolled oats
60g/2oz/½ cup lucuma powder
60g/2oz/½ cup mesquite powder
6 whole strawberries, to serve

1 Put the cacao butter in a large heatproof bowl set over a pan of barely simmering water. When melted, remove the bowl from the heat.

Lucuma powder is the most popular flavour for ice cream in many Latin American countries

2 Discard the soaking water from the cashews and put them in a blender. Add the melted cacao butter, avocados, strawberries, maple syrup, lemon juice and vanilla. Blend on high for about 30 seconds until combined. Add a little water, if needed.

3 Pour the creamy mixture into six dessert glasses.

4 Drain the almonds, then process them in a food processor with the oats to make the crumbly topping.

5 Transfer the almond mixture to a mixing bowl, add the lucuma and mesquite, then stir in 30ml/2 tbsp cold water with a fork to form some crumbly clumps.

6 Spoon the crumbly topping evenly over the parfaits, top each dessert with a strawberry and chill until ready to serve.

Sweetened with apple juice and cinnamon, this dessert is gentle and healthy for you and your family. The berries give it a beautiful colour as well as adding pectin for a more jelly-like texture. Use fresh or frozen berries, as seasonally available. It is best to prepare this dessert a day ahead of serving because the chia seeds will form a gel in about 10 minutes, but the longer they are soaked, the more bioavailable the nutrients become.

It's up to personal preference whether you choose to serve the pudding as it is, or blended until the texture is smooth. All the health benefits of the chia gel are still present in the smooth dessert, which is perhaps a little more elegant for a dinner party.

Apple Chia Puddings

SERVES 6
115g/4oz/1 cup blackberries,
   blueberries or blackcurrants
5ml/1 tsp ground cinnamon, to taste
750ml/1¼ pints/3 cups apple juice
15ml/1 tbsp honey, to sweeten
  (optional)
150g/5oz/1 cup chia seeds
fresh berries and mint sprigs,
   to decorate (optional)

1 Put the berries, cinnamon and juice in a blender and blend on high until combined. If the apple juice is tart, add a tablespoon of honey to sweeten to taste, if liked.

2 Put the berry mixture in a bowl with the chia, whisking with a fork to make sure the chia seeds are moistened.

3 Leave to soak for at least 10 minutes, or overnight in the refrigerator, if possible.

4 When you're ready to serve, spoon the chia pudding into six dessert glasses as it is, or if preferred, blend for about 15–30 seconds until smooth before serving. Decorate with fresh berries and sprigs of mint, if liked.

Soaked chia seeds slowly release fluid into your body over time, keeping you hydrated for longer

Jellies, Mousses and Soufflés

Jellies, Mousses and Soufflés

There's a lot of interest in bone broth at the moment as a consequence of paleo dietary ideas, and it is undeniable that it has many health benefits. Make sure you buy unflavoured, natural gelatine that specifies it was made humanely. I recommend a brand called Great Lakes. It's available in the UK and USA and can be found in stores and online. While it's not certified as organic, it is from a small family farm that raises cattle humanely.

If you can find Concord grape juice, all the better. Concord grapes are a variety that are native to the United States, and taste much more fragrant than standard red grapes. They have about double the amount of antioxidants in them than regular red grapes.

Grape Jellies

SERVES 6
4 unflavoured gelatine leaves,
    cut into quarters
400ml/14fl oz/1⅔ cups red grape juice
a bunch of grapes, halved and
    deseeded, to serve

If you're not vegetarian, it's time to rediscover jelly. It's fun to pour it into a silicone ice cube mould for individual cubes of jelly

1 Soak the gelatine in the juice for 5–10 minutes in a measuring jug or cup.

2 Remove the soaked gelatine from the juice, gently squeeze out the liquid and reserve the leaves.

3 Put the juice in a pan and heat slowly until very warm but not boiling. Remove from the heat after about 10 minutes and add the gelatine leaves. Stir until all of the gelatine has dissolved.

4 Pour the gelatine mixture into six individual silicone moulds, pouring very slowly to avoid making air bubbles. Carefully transfer the jellies to the refrigerator to set for at least 8 hours, or overnight. Allow 24 hours for very firm jellies.

5 To remove the jellies from the moulds, wet six serving plates so that you'll be able to reposition your jelly once it's turned out. Fill a bowl with warm water, and suspend the bottom and sides of each of the silicone moulds in the water for about 2–3 seconds.

6 Hold the mould upside down over each serving plate and turn the jelly out. Move the jelly around on the plate so that it's in the perfect position, then serve immediately, or chill in the refrigerator for up to 8 hours, until ready to serve.

7 Decorate the individual jellies with fresh grapes before serving, arranging them around the base of each jelly.

These fresh and fruity jellies are elegant served at any time of day. They are completely vegan, as they are made using agar instead of gelatine. Agar is an extract of red algae, which is used to stabilize foams, thicken sauces or gel liquids. It's full of minerals and perfect for the no-sugar cook, as it is rich in soluble fibre and absorbs glucose in the stomach, helping to stabilize blood sugar. A great recipe for a last-minute dessert, these only take half an hour to set and will hold their shape at room temperature.

Vegan Strawberry Jellies

SERVES 10
450g/1lb/2 cups fresh strawberries, hulled
75ml/2½fl oz/⅓ cup maple syrup
500ml/17fl oz/generous 2 cups cold water
75ml/2½fl oz/⅓ cup lime juice
5ml/1 tsp agar powder or 15ml/ 1 tbsp agar flakes
0.5ml/⅛ tsp locust bean gum

1 Slice half the strawberries and combine them with 15ml/1 tbsp of the maple syrup in a bowl. Set aside to macerate for 30 minutes.

2 Put the rest of the strawberries in a blender with the water. Blend on high until liquid.

3 Pass the liquidized strawberries through a sieve or strainer lined with muslin or cheesecloth, crushing with a spoon to remove any remaining solids.

4 Rinse the blender with water, then add the blended and strained strawberries and all of the remaining ingredients. Blend for a few seconds to combine.

5 Put the strawberry mixture in a pan and slowly bring to the boil over a medium heat, stirring regularly. Lower the heat and allow to simmer, uncovered, for 3–5 minutes, stirring regularly. If using agar flakes instead of powder, simmer for 10–15 minutes.

6 Put the macerated whole strawberries into the bottom of 10 coupé glasses. Pour the jelly mixture over the top, and leave to set in the refrigerator for half an hour. Serve chilled.

I've included locust bean gum to help create a smooth texture, and maple syrup because the malty maple flavour is a perfect partner for strawberries

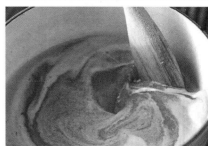

These rich and comforting custards never fail to bring the sunshine back with their lemony snicketty goodness. Naturally sweetened with dates, there is a richness to the flavour that is perfectly balanced with the sharpness of the lemon. They're traditional and not-so-traditional... just like the times we live in. Make them ahead of time so they are waiting for you to whisk out of the refrigerator and serve in a jiffy.

Cold Lemon Custards

SERVES 4
10 stoned (pitted) dates, chopped
500ml/17fl oz/generous 2 cups full
   cream (whole) milk
40g/1½oz/⅓ cup cornflour (cornstarch)
1.5ml/¼ tsp sea salt
grated rind of 1 lemon
1 egg, lightly beaten

1 Put the dates in a bowl with 30ml/ 2 tbsp boiling water and set aside to soak.

2 Put 450ml/¾ pint/scant 2 cups of the milk in a heatproof bowl set over a large pan of barely simmering water. Do not let the surface of the bowl touch the water. Gently heat the milk, stirring continuously, so that no skin forms.

3 Put the cornflour and salt in a separate small bowl, then add the remaining milk little by little. Blend thoroughly using a metal spoon, crushing any lumps.

4 When the milk in the heatproof bowl is hot and steaming but not boiling, add the cornflour mixture. Keep stirring until the warm milk has thickened, then cover with a lid. Cook over a low heat for about 10 minutes.

5 Put the lemon rind in a small mixing bowl. Add the egg and the dates with their soaking liquid and mix to combine. Pour the mixture into the hot milk and stir until incorporated.

6 Cook for 2–3 minutes more, stirring constantly, until the custard has heated, combined and thickened. Pour into four ramekins and chill for at least 1 hour before serving.

Naturally sweetened with dates, there is a richness to the flavour that is perfectly balanced with the sharpness of the lemon.
Use standard-sized dates, or reduce the quantity if using larger fancy ones like Medjool

Pears are one of my favourite fruits, but they are only ripe for a fleeting moment before they become over-ripe. After this point, the texture becomes mealy and soft, so it's tempting to throw them on to the compost, despite knowing they are at their sweetest and best in terms of flavour.

However, there is no need for your over-ripe pears to go to waste with this light and fluffy soufflé recipe. It makes the most of their sweet, delicate flavour and their soft texture. In fact, for these soufflés, the softer the pears, the better the result will be!

Pear Soufflés

SERVES 6
15ml/1 tbsp unsalted butter,
   for greasing
450g/1lb/2 cups over-ripe pears,
   peeled and cored
grated rind and juice of 1 large orange
100g/3¾oz/scant 1 cup agave powder,
   plus extra for sprinkling
2.5ml/½ tsp ground cinnamon
3 egg whites

There is no need for your over-ripe pears to go to waste with this light and fluffy soufflé recipe. It makes the most of their sweet, delicate flavour

1 Grease six 150ml/¼ pint/⅔ cup ramekins with butter.

2 Put the pears in a large pan with a lid. Add the orange rind and juice.

3 Put the agave powder in a bowl. Mix in the cinnamon and add 50g/2oz/½ cup of the mixture to the pan with the pears.

4 Cook the pears over a medium heat, stirring frequently, for about 5 minutes until combined. Remove from the heat, purée completely with a hand-held blender and set aside to cool.

5 When you're ready to bake the soufflés, put a baking sheet (with sides) in the oven, and heat it to 200°C/400°F/Gas 6.

6 Spoon 30ml/2 tbsp of the pear purée into each of the ramekins.

7 Put the egg whites in a large metal or glass mixing bowl and whisk on high with an electric whisk until they form stiff peaks.

8 Fold the egg whites into the remaining agave powder mixture and mix with the rest of the pear purée very gently.

9 Spoon the pear and egg white mixture into the ramekins and level the tops of the soufflés using a palette knife. Run your thumb or a knife around the inside of each ramekin before baking.

10 Remove the hot baking sheet from the oven. Put the ramekins on the baking sheet and bake immediately for about 12 minutes until the soufflés have risen beyond the ramekins and the tops are golden brown. Dust with agave powder and serve immediately.

Zabaglione is traditionally made with marsala wine, but as it contains a high percentage of sugar, I created a recipe to allow sugar-free enjoyment of this lovely dessert. Vodka is sugar free, so it can be used in many recipes as a substitute for drinks that contain sugar. Of course, vodka doesn't have the same sweetness or flavour as marsala wine, so here it is mixed with honey to create an alternative that works perfectly with the egg yolks.

All soft fruit work well with zabaglione, including summer berries and ripe peaches, but I've chosen mango for this recipe because its fragrant flavour evokes a little of the marsala taste. Serve with sugar-free almond cookies, such as the florentines on page 172.

Zabaglione with Mango

SERVES 4
1 ripe mango
3 egg yolks
45ml/3 tbsp honey
25ml/1½ tbsp vodka
25ml/1½ tbsp warm water
2.5ml/½ tsp brandy extract (optional)

1 Peel the mango, remove the stone (pit) with a sharp knife and dice the flesh. Put half the mango cubes into four dessert glasses, and set the rest aside.

2 Put all the other ingredients in a heatproof bowl and whisk together using a hand-held blender with a whisk attachment, or an electric whisk set on high, until combined.

3 Set the bowl over a pan of barely simmering water, holding it in place with an oven glove. Heat the mixture, whisking continuously, until lukewarm.

4 Remove the bowl from the heat, still whisking. After 30 seconds, put the bowl back over the heat and continue to whisk until warm and thickened to the consistency of eggnog, but no more.

5 Remove the zabaglione from the heat. Pour half of it equally over the mango in the four dessert glasses, then add a second layer of mango and finish with a second layer of zabaglione. Allow to cool before serving.

Guaranteed to be a delicious talking point at your next dinner party, this chocolate dessert is vegan as well as no-sugar. Chocolate is made out of cacao beans, which are the nuts inside the cacao fruit. These nuts are actually good for you – the real reason most chocolate is bad for you is the sugar.

This recipe is sweetened with stevia, which works well as the intense flavours of the raw cacao and espresso powder are robust enough to handle its mixed sweet and bitter flavours. The coconut cream needs to chill overnight in the refrigerator, so start preparing this a day ahead of serving.

Chocolate Espresso Mousses

SERVES 6
160ml/5½fl oz can coconut cream, chilled overnight in the refrigerator
2 ripe avocados
60ml/4 tbsp cacao powder
30ml/2 tbsp instant espresso coffee powder
5ml/1 tsp dried stevia powder or 10ml/2 tsp granulated stevia
a handful of fresh blueberries and sprigs of mint, to decorate (optional)

1 Drain the coconut cream and discard any liquid. Put the hardened cream in a blender.

2 Add all the other ingredients and blend until smooth.

3 Spoon the mousse into six espresso cups, and chill in the refrigerator for at least 2 hours, or overnight.

4 Serve decorated with blueberries and sprigs of mint, if liked.

Ice Cream, Snow Cones and Ice Pops

Whether vegan or dairy, these frozen desserts can be whipped up at a moment's notice to satisfy your craving for no-sugar sweetness at the drop of a sun hat. Go figgy in the summer, reach for the pomegranates in the autumn, or crush the winter blues with bitter orange! There are frozen fancies here for every season, whether served on their own, or as an accompaniment to another no-sugar dessert from the book.

Freezing different liquids produces many different textures. Whether dairy cream or nut milk, an emulsion produces a delicate smoothness that melts slowly on the tongue, releasing flavours drop by drop

Ice cream has to contain some sort of oil – that's the difference between a sorbet and a true ice cream. However, with this luscious recipe, the dairy cream content is halved by adding almonds. The oils in the almonds keep it creamy while allowing it to be less heavy.

As with all ice cream recipes, it's best to remove this from the freezer and allow to soften before serving. However, you can also defrost it completely, as it's delicious served at room temperature as a mousse. Feel free to skip step 1 if you already have some almond milk made up. I find it is always handy to keep some in the refrigerator ready to use.

Chocolate and Almond Ice Cream

SERVES 12

25g/1oz/¼ cup almonds, soaked in water for at least 5 hours or overnight in the refrigerator
120ml/4fl oz/½ cup water
120ml/4fl oz/¼ cup agave syrup
40g/1½oz/½ cup raw cacao powder
50g/2oz/½ cup Peruvian carob or mesquite powder
750ml/1¼ pints/3 cups double (heavy) cream
115g/4oz/1 cup chopped almonds

1 Put the soaked almonds and water in a blender and blend on high until well mixed. Strain the liquid into a bowl using a sieve or strainer lined with a piece of muslin or cheesecloth. Squeeze the muslin to extract as much of the liquid as possible, then discard the remaining pulp.

2 Add the agave syrup to the almond milk, then sift the cacao and carob into the bowl. Add the cream, then put the mixture back into the blender and blend until combined.

3 Put the ice cream mixture in a freezerproof container and stir in the chopped almonds. Cover with the lid and freeze for 2–3 hours. Remove the container from the freezer and set aside for about 20 minutes to thaw slightly, then stir and mash the ice cream with a metal spoon to break up the ice crystals. When smooth, cover the container with the lid and return to the freezer.

4 After 2–3 hours, repeat this process, then cover the ice cream first with a layer of wax paper, cut to size, and then with the lid. Return to the freezer until ready to serve. The ice cream will store for up to 6 months.

Fresh figs are summer's softest fruit, velvet-coated and naturally sweet. Paired with Mediterranean-style honey such as orange blossom, lavender or lemon honey, they have the power to evoke warmer climes like no other fruit.

In this recipe, fresh figs are steeped overnight and then poached in honey to make a smooth ice cream that doesn't need to be churned. Try making it with goat's cream to add a luxurious dimension to this special summer recipe. Serve with plain wafer biscuits or cookies and fresh mint tea in a shady spot in the garden.

Fresh Fig Ice Cream

SERVES 10
10 fresh figs, chopped into
    bite-sized chunks
150ml/¼ pint/⅔ cup honey
500ml/17fl oz/generous 2 cups double
    (heavy) cream, chilled
5 egg yolks

1 Steep the figs in the honey overnight in the refrigerator. The next day, put them in a pan over a medium heat and bring to the boil. Cook for about 3 minutes until soft.

2 Pour the cream into a mixing bowl and whisk until it forms stiff peaks, then chill in the refrigerator.

3 Beat the egg yolks in a separate bowl using an electric whisk, or in a food processor, for about 2 minutes until pale yellow. Continue beating and drizzle the warm honey and fig mixture into the yolks slowly, then whisk all the ingredients together on high for 5 minutes.

4 Take the cream out of the refrigerator and gently fold it into the fig, honey and egg mixture using a silicone spatula.

5 Put the ice cream in a storage container, cover and freeze for about 2 hours, until set.

This lovely vegan ice cream is very healthy, although not strictly raw, as it is made with cashews. Like all nuts, cashews grow inside a fruit. Between the nut and the fruit is a thin membrane that's poisonous. It makes it hard to separate the nuts from the fruit because it brings out an acute allergic reaction in the skin. In order to ensure cashews are safe to handle and consume, they are steamed in boiling water meaning they are never really raw, despite any wording on the label. Make sure you use nuts that are as uncooked as possible for this recipe. If you use unsalted and unroasted cashews, they'll soak up lots of water, and will make a perfectly creamy, dreamy ice cream.

Cashew and Almond Ice Cream

SERVES 12

225g/8oz/2 cups cashew nuts
500ml/17fl oz/generous 2 cups
  coconut water
215g/7½oz/1 cup coconut oil, melted
125ml/4fl oz/½ cup clear honey
30g/1¼oz/¼ cup sun-dried cane
  crystals
10ml/2 tsp ground vanilla pods (beans)
5ml/1 tsp vanilla extract
2.5ml/½ tsp sea salt
flaked (sliced) almonds, to serve
  (optional)

1 Soak the cashews in cold water for at least 1 hour, or up to 4 hours, at room temperature. Drain the liquid and discard the soaking water.

2 Put the soaked cashews in a blender with all the other ingredients and blend on high for 3 minutes.

3 Put the mixture in a freezerproof container, cover with a sheet of baking parchment cut to size, and freeze for 4 hours. The ice cream will store for up to 6 months.

4 Remove from the freezer half an hour before serving, to soften. Serve in sundae glasses topped with flaked almonds, if liked.

These iced lollies are perfect for children's parties and can be made in minutes! If you don't have much time, just use fresh berries without macerating. However, steeping the berries in honey breaks down their texture as well as adding sweetness, which is always a little lacking in store-bought berries.

Coconut Berry Popsicles

MAKES 10
300g/11oz/2¾ cups mixed berries, eg strawberries, raspberries, blackberries
60ml/4 tbsp clear honey (optional)
250ml/8fl oz/1 cup fresh or carton coconut water
10 iced lolly (popsicle) sticks

1 Hull all the berries and slice the strawberries, if using, into 5mm/¼in thick slices.

2 Put the berries in a shallow dish and drizzle with the honey, if using. Pour the coconut water over the top and leave to macerate in the refrigerator for at least half an hour, or up to 24 hours.

3 When you're ready to make the popsicles, gently remove the berries from the liquid with a fork.

4 Drop the berries one by one into a 10 popsicle mould, layering them so that the flat sides of the strawberries are pressed up against the edges of the mould. Arrange any whole berries like raspberries carefully to show them off as much as possible in the sides of the mould, and from top to bottom.

5 When all of the berries are in the moulds, carefully pour the liquid in to fill them, using a funnel if necessary.

6 Insert the sticks, and freeze for at least 1 hour. The popsicles will keep in the moulds for up to 6 months.

Treat yourself to the raw water direct from a fresh coconut

Incredibly simple and with double the nutrition of regular orange iced lollies, these citrus treats are made with the rind of the orange as well as the juice to make the most of the nutrients contained in the whole fruit. Every time you eat an orange, it's fun to see if you can find a way to enjoy the zest. It makes better sense in terms of your weekly food budget, and simultaneously in terms of your quest to enjoy a more flavoursome approach to cuisine.

Yacons are a kind of yam, which is a natural companion to oranges in the classic American Thanksgiving meal. The yacon flavour blends beautifully with the orange juice and rind, and supports the body's natural digestive processes.

Bitter Orange Popsicles

MAKES 10
2 medium oranges
30ml/2 tbsp yacon syrup
750ml/1¼ pints/3 cups water
10 iced lolly (popsicle) sticks

1 Grate the rind of the oranges into thin strips using a zesting tool (citrus grater), then put the rind in a blender.

2 Cut the oranges in half and squeeze as much juice as possible into the blender. Add the yacon syrup and the water, then blend on high for about 1 minute.

3 Pour the liquid into a 10 popsicle mould, insert the sticks and freeze for at least 4 hours. The popsicles will keep in the moulds for up to 6 months.

These vegan creamsicles taste like banana custard, but they don't contain eggs. Using banana flakes instead of fresh bananas, they can be made from scratch quickly in any season. The flakes are made from ripe red bananas, a sweet variety that's very hard to find fresh. It's much higher in phytonutrients than the most widespread variety of fresh bananas, and has a rounder, almost caramelized flavour.

In this recipe, hemp seeds are whizzed with water to become a milk substitute. Its luxuriously creamy texture makes these creamsicles silky, but still compactly frozen and easy to eat. Use hulled hemp seeds, not whole, as the hulls are too tough to make creamy milk without straining the liquid.

Banana Creamsicles

MAKES 8
50g/2oz/½ cup hemp seed hearts
115g/4oz/1 cup banana flakes
350ml/12fl oz/1½ cups cold water
8 iced lolly (popsicle) sticks

1 Put all the ingredients in a blender. Blend for about 30 seconds–1 minute on high, until the seeds have completely liquidized and blended with the other ingredients.

2 Pour the liquid into an 8 popsicle mould, insert the sticks and freeze overnight. These creamsicles can be frozen and stored in the mould for a few months.

As with all berries, pomegranates are rich in phytonutrients and antioxidants, making these snow cones as nutritious as they are delicious. If possible, make the crushed ice using a high-speed blender, but if you don't have one the same recipe can be used to make popsicles.

Pomegranate Snow Cones

SERVES 4
4 medium pomegranates
30ml/2 tbsp clear honey or barley
  malt syrup
250ml/8fl oz/1 cup cold water

1 Remove the edible flesh from the pomegranates and put it in a metal sieve or strainer suspended over a glass or metal bowl. Press the fruit through with the back of a metal spoon to release the juice. It will yield about 500ml/17fl oz/generous 2 cups of juice. Continue this process until all that's left in the sieve or strainer are the seeds. Alternatively, juice the pomegranates using a juicer. Discard the seeds.

2 Add the honey or barley malt syrup to the pomegranate juice and mix, using a metal spoon, to combine.

3 Pour the liquid into an ice cube tray, and freeze for at least 1 hour, or overnight.

4 When you're ready to serve the snow cones, put the pomegranate ice cubes into a high-speed blender. Blend on high for a few seconds, but no longer. Spoon the pomegranate ice into four martini glasses and serve immediately.

Pomegranate juice is highly pigmented, so it's full of natural nutrition, but these snow cones should be eaten with paper napkins to hand

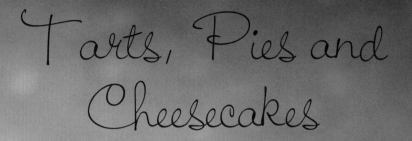

Tarts, Pies and Cheesecakes

Elegant at times and messy at others, these tarts, pies and cheesecakes are thoroughly modern for the most part, with a nod to the traditional. There is no need to give up eating classic desserts such as these just because you've given up eating sugar. Whether a fruit pie or a cheesecake, they're perfect shared with company at teatime, or at the end of a beautiful dinner party with friends and family.

These delicious tarts and pies are pure, raw creaminess floating above a base of crumbliness, each complementing the other without a grain of sugar in sight!

A chocolate tart crust with a creamy chocolate filling... and all without any sugar, dairy or gluten! This raw vegan paleo recipe is every bit as good as a baked chocolate tart, but far less fussy to make and a million times healthier.

Its dark brown chocolate colour makes a fabulous backdrop for decoration. Try finishing it with organic, raw, edible toppings such as rose petals, fresh berries, sliced almonds, or piped cashew cream for a classic, elegant look. Or let your imagination run wild and decorate it with non-edibles, like birthday candles, faux flowers, tiny strings of bunting cut from felt and suspended on bamboo skewers, or any other decorations that take your fancy! Start preparation a day before serving, as it is best to soak the cashew nuts overnight.

Chocolate Avocado Cream Tart

SERVES 8

For the pastry:
115g/4oz/1 cup cashew nuts, soaked in water for at least 4 hours or overnight
40g/1½oz/½ cup oats
75g/3oz/½ cup macadamia nuts
60g/2¼oz/¾ cup cacao powder
5ml/1 tsp vanilla extract
75g/3oz/about 14 dried stoned (pitted) dates

For the filling:
2 ripe avocados
60ml/4 tbsp cacao powder
30ml/2 tbsp clear honey
mixed fresh berries, to decorate

1 To make the pastry, drain the cashew nuts and put them in a food processor with the oats, macadamias, cacao and vanilla. Pulse until broken down and combined, add the dates and process again to make a dough.

2 Press the dough into a 25cm/10in diameter round flan tin or pan, flattening it into the bottom and up the sides of the tin using the back of a spoon. Put it in the freezer for 20 minutes to set.

3 When the pastry case or pie shell is ready, make the creamy filling. Halve the avocados, remove the stones (pits) and scoop the flesh into a blender. Add the cacao and honey and blend for about 20 seconds on high to combine.

4 Pour the filling into the pastry case, cover and leave to set in the refrigerator for at least 20 minutes, but preferably for a few hours or overnight. Keep covered until ready to eat, then decorate with a selection of fresh berries, before serving.

A chocolate tart crust with a creamy chocolate filling...
and all without any sugar, dairy or gluten!
Try topping it with organic, raw, edible decorations

This is my classic recipe for a raw cashew cream pie. Here, it is flavoured with vanilla and lime, but there's no limit to the different ways you can explore flavours with this simple nut cream base. Go floral, with rose water or orange blossom water, or with a drop of lavender essential oil, or rose otto. Go spicy, with a pinch of cayenne and some chai tea, or with fresh ginger and turmeric. Chocolate is always an option, of course, and seasonal fruits never fail to bring smiles to everyone's faces, whether they're incorporated into the cream topping, like the lime in this recipe, or used to decorate the top.

Start preparing this the day before serving as the cashew nuts and dates must be soaked in water overnight.

Cashew Lime Pie

SERVES 8

For the pastry:
100g/3¾oz/1½ cups dried, shredded coconut
50g/2oz/½ cup ground almonds

For the filling:
grated rind and juice of 1 lime
225g/8oz/2 cups raw cashew nuts, soaked in water overnight
15ml/1 tbsp ground vanilla pods (beans)
8 dried stoned (pitted) dates, soaked in water overnight
thin strips of lime rind, to decorate

1 To make the pastry, put the coconut and ground almonds in a mixing bowl and stir with a spoon to combine. Add the soaking water from the dates little by little, until the dough sticks together.

2 Press the dough into a 23cm/9in diameter round pie tin or pan lined with baking parchment. Flatten it into the bottom and up the sides of the tin using the back of a spoon. Chill in the refrigerator for at least 1 hour while you prepare the filling.

3 To make the filling, put the lime rind and juice in a blender. Drain the cashew nuts, discarding the soaking water, and add them to the blender with the vanilla and dates. Reserve the soaking water from the dates and set aside.

4 Blend on low, building up to medium. Stop the blender now and then to mix the cashew paste using a silicone spatula and add the date soaking water little by little, if needed, to keep the consistency creamy. Repeat until the mixture is a smooth nut cream, adding more date soaking water if necessary.

5 Remove the pastry case or pie shell from the refrigerator. Pour in the filling and smooth with a palette knife until evenly distributed, then chill for at least 1 hour to set. Decorate with thin strips of lime rind before serving.

Add strawberries when you purée the cashew nuts to make a strawberry cashew cream pie

This deliciously creamy pie is as tempting as any other treat in the book, but it's quick to make, requires zero baking and is decadent as well as good for you! Because this pie is made with coconut and almonds, it can be prepared with much less soaking time than many other raw creamy nut pies. By chopping the almonds before they are soaked, the soaking time is minimized. Use fresh coconut water if making a raw pie, otherwise any good canned coconut water is fine.

Serve it as a part of a special tea party, or at the end of a dinner party. If you like almonds and coconut, you'll love it!

Coconut Almond Cream Pie

SERVES 24

For the pastry:
185g/6½oz/2½ cups dried, shredded coconut
75g/3oz/¾ cup ground almonds
6–8 fresh or dried stoned (pitted) dates
30–60ml/2–3 tbsp clear honey
2.5ml/½ tsp cinnamon
1.5ml/¼ tsp ground nutmeg
1.5ml/¼ tsp ground cardamom
2.5ml/½ tsp ground vanilla pods (beans)
1.5ml/¼ tsp sea salt

For the filling:
50g/2oz/½ cup chopped almonds, soaked in water for 1 hour in the refrigerator
water and flesh from 1 fresh young Thai coconut or raw fresh coconut water and canned coconut cream
30ml/2 tbsp raw agave syrup
30ml/2 tbsp coconut oil, melted
7.5ml/1½ tsp ground vanilla pods (beans)
mixed berries, to serve

1 Line a 23 x 33cm/9 x 13in cake tin or pan with baking parchment.

2 To make the pastry, put the coconut in a food processor and process until coarsely ground. Add the ground almonds, dates, honey, spices, vanilla and salt, and process for about 3 minutes to make a cookie-style dough. Add more honey, if needed, to make the dough stick together.

3 Press the dough into the prepared cake tin or pan, flattening it into the bottom using the back of a spoon.

4 To make the filling, drain the soaked almonds, discarding the soaking liquid, and put them in a blender. Add the coconut water and blend for 3 minutes on high.

5 Strain the mixture through a sieve or strainer lined with muslin, cheesecloth or fine nylon mesh fabric set over a large bowl and squeeze the fabric to extract any remaining liquid from the ground nuts into the bowl.

6 Rinse the blender and pour the almond coconut water mixture back into it. Add the coconut flesh, agave, coconut oil and vanilla, and blend on high for about 1 minute to combine.

7 Pour the filling over the pastry and smooth with a palette knife. Chill the pie in the refrigerator for at least 1 hour before serving, or overnight if preparing in advance. Decorate with a selection of fresh berries, if liked, then serve.

Sometimes, simple is best. Pears are such delicate fruit when they are ripe, so to enjoy their texture, pair them with this soft crust-less cheesecake. Choose the mildest young goat's cheese to add just a hint of acidity to the finished cake. Start preparing this a day ahead of serving as the cheesecake needs to set overnight in the refrigerator. The pears will be sweeter and more delicious if left to macerate overnight as well.

Pear and Goat's Cheesecake

SERVES 12

3 ripe pears, peeled, cored and sliced
175ml/6fl oz/¾ cup honey
2.5ml/½ tsp ground cinnamon
1.5ml/¼ tsp ground nutmeg
450g/16oz/2 cups cream cheese,
   at room temperature
225g/8oz/1 cup mascarpone,
   at room temperature
115g/4oz/½ cup goat's cheese,
   at room temperature
5ml/1 tsp vanilla extract
1.5ml/¼ tsp sea salt
3 eggs

1 Drizzle the pears with 50ml/2fl oz/¼ cup of the honey, add the spices and set aside to macerate for at least half an hour, or preferably overnight.

2 Preheat the oven to 180°C/350°F/Gas 4.

3 Cream the cheeses, vanilla, salt and the remaining honey together in a mixing bowl using an electric whisk on medium for about 5 minutes, until fluffy and combined.

4 Whisk in the eggs one by one, incorporating each one before adding the next.

5 Pour the batter into a 23cm/9in diameter springform cake tin or pan, and bake the cake for about 50 minutes, until it has risen around the sides, the top is brown, and it's still moist and not entirely firm in the middle.

6 Allow to cool in the tin on a wire rack, then transfer to the refrigerator, and allow the cake to continue to set overnight.

7 The next day, pour the macerating juices from the pears over the cake and decorate the top with the pear slices. Chill in the refrigerator for 4 hours before serving.

Pears are such delicate fruit — to enjoy their texture, pair them with this soft, crust-less cheesecake

I grew up in London, but I've always loved New York-style blueberry cheesecake. The problem is, it's usually incredibly sweet. In this recipe, all of the refined sugar is removed and it is much lighter in fat than most because it's made with ricotta. The crust is made from walnuts and dates, which creates a healthier and more modern feel for this classic dessert. It's elegant and perfect to serve in your garden on a summer's night.

Three different natural, unrefined sweeteners are used here to bring this cheesecake together perfectly. The raw cane crystals help the top of the cake brown as it bakes. The dates add stickiness to the base and the honey softens the blueberries as their juices transform from tart to delicious.

Blueberry Cheesecake

SERVES 12

For the base:
150g/5oz/1 cup fresh or dried stoned (pitted) dates
115g/4oz/1 cup chopped walnuts, soaked in water overnight in the refrigerator

For the filling:
1kg/2¼lb/4 cups fresh blueberries
45ml/3 tbsp honey
1kg/2¼lb/4 cups ricotta cheese
150g/5oz/1 cup raw cane crystals
5ml/1 tsp grated lemon rind
10ml/2 tsp vanilla extract
1.5ml/¼ tsp sea salt
4 eggs

1 Preheat the oven to 180°C/350°F/Gas 4.

2 To make the base, soak the dates in warm water for 10 minutes.

3 Drain the dates and discard the soaking liquid. Put them in a food processor with the drained, soaked walnuts and process for about 30 seconds until combined.

4 Press the walnut and date mixture into the bottom of a 23cm/9in springform cake tin or pan with the back of a spoon and chill while you prepare the filling.

5 Mix the blueberries with the honey and set aside to macerate.

6 Put the ricotta, cane crystals, lemon rind, vanilla and salt in a mixing bowl and beat with an electric whisk for 2 minutes on medium until combined.

7 Whisk in the eggs one by one, incorporating each one before adding the next.

8 Pour the batter over the base and bake for about 1 hour, until the cake has risen around the sides, the top is brown and it's still moist and not entirely firm in the middle. Allow to cool in the tin on a wire rack.

9 Remove the outer ring from the tin and pour the macerating juices from the blueberries over the cake. Decorate the top with the blueberries and allow to stand at room temperature for about 20 minutes before serving.

Elegant and perfect to serve in your garden on a summer's night

Gluten-free, sugar-free and dairy-free, this fresh peach tart is summery and incredibly luscious. Gone are the days when healthy meant not very nice! This tart proves the point, as it's beyond gorgeous, and is also easy peasy to make.

The pastry can be made on the day, or up to three days in advance if that suits your schedule, but it's definitely best to assemble the pastry base and the rest of the tart on the day of serving to avoid the pastry becoming too moist.

If you'd prefer to make a raw version of this dessert, simply replace the coconut cream with raw dairy cream if you can find it, or with a small, ripe avocado that's mashed with the excess honey marinade after the fruit has been macerated.

Peach Tart

SERVES 9

For the filling:
30ml/2 tbsp honey
2.5ml/½ tsp ground cinnamon
4 ripe peaches
160ml/5½fl oz can coconut cream, poured into a mixing bowl and chilled or 1 large ripe avocado
2.5ml/½ tsp cinnamon, to serve

For the pastry:
115g/4oz/1 cup walnuts, almonds or pecans, chilled in the freezer
150g/5oz/2 cups dried, shredded coconut
10 dried pitted dates, soaked for 1 hour in 50ml/2fl oz/¼ cup boiling water

1 Grease a 20cm x 20cm/8in x 8in square cake tin or pan and line with baking parchment.

2 To make the filling, mix the honey and cinnamon with 15ml/1 tbsp warm water to create a marinade.

3 Remove the stones (pits) from the peaches and slice them into 10–12 segments per fruit.

4 Put the sliced peaches in a shallow dish, drizzle with the honey mixture, and set aside to macerate in the refrigerator for 1 hour.

5 To make the pastry, put the nuts in a food processor and pulse for 1–2 minutes. Add the shredded coconut and pulse for about 10 seconds until broken down and combined. Add the dates in their soaking liquid and pulse for about 2 minutes to form a paste. Remove the blade and mix with your hands if it's too sticky to process.

6 Press the date mixture into the bottom of the prepared baking tin or pan with the back of a spoon. Set aside in the refrigerator for at least 1 hour.

7 When the tart is ready to assemble, remove the coconut cream from the refrigerator and put it in a mixing bowl. Whip the coconut cream for about 2 minutes with an electric whisk on low, slowly increasing the speed. The colder the cream, the fluffier it will become when whipped.

8 Spread the whipped coconut cream evenly over the pastry case or pie shell, using a silicone spatula.

9 Alternatively, if using avocado instead of coconut cream, put the avocado in a bowl and mash with a fork. Add the macerating juices, mix until combined and spread evenly over the pastry. Cover with an even layer of peach slices.

10 Chill the tart in the refrigerator for at least 1 hour to set, but remove 1 hour before serving and bring to room temperature. Lift the whole tart out of the tin or pan using the baking parchment and slide it off of the paper and on to a serving platter.

11 Sprinkle with cinnamon and serve. The tart will keep in the refrigerator for up to 3 days.

Perhaps my favourite dessert from childhood, this British regional tart has been reimagined here without sugar or gluten and with fresh fruit instead of jam.

There's plenty of butter in the pastry and the frangipane filling is made with eggs so this isn't a vegan dessert, and it's certainly not low in calories. However, it's undeniably modern and aligned to the way we eat now, while retaining its traditional Englishness. Perfect for teatime.

Summer Bakewell Tart

SERVES 12
For the filling:
250g/9oz/2 cups raspberries, fresh or defrosted from frozen
30ml/2 tbsp agave syrup

For the pastry:
60g/2¼oz/⅓ cup brown rice flour, plus extra for dusting
30g/1¼oz/¼ cup oat flour
50g/2oz/⅓ cup potato starch
0.6ml/⅛ tsp sea salt
80g/3¼oz/6½ tbsp unsalted butter, frozen
iced water, to mix

For the frangipane:
15ml/1 tbsp rice flour
5ml/1 tsp oat flour
15ml/1 tbsp potato starch
115g/4oz/1 cup ground almonds
2.5ml/½ tsp bicarbonate of soda (baking soda)

115g/4oz/½ cup unsalted butter, at room temperature, plus extra for greasing
115g/4oz/¾ cup coconut crystals
1.5ml/¼ tsp almond extract
2 eggs
flaked (sliced) almonds and fresh raspberries, to serve

1 To make the filling, mix the raspberries and agave syrup together in a small bowl. Set aside in the refrigerator to macerate.

2 To make the pastry, sift the flours, potato starch and salt into a mixing bowl. Grate the butter into the bowl using a box grater, then mix it into the flour with your hands without rubbing it in, adding a little water as you do so. Keep adding the water until the dough is wet enough to hold together in a ball, but not sticky.

3 Bring the dough together in a ball and cover with clear film (plastic wrap). Chill for at least 1 hour, or overnight.

4 When you're ready to make the tart, preheat the oven to 190°C/375°F/Gas 5. Grease a 23cm/9in diameter flan tin or pan with butter and line the bottom with baking parchment.

5 Dust the counter with rice flour, then roll out the pastry to a circle of about 30cm/12in diameter. Transfer the pastry to the tin with the rolling pin, cut away any excess, and line the top of the pastry with another circle of baking parchment. Weigh it down with dry beans, and bake for 10 minutes.

6 To make the frangipane, sift the rice and oat flours, potato starch, ground almonds and bicarbonate of soda into a bowl.

▶

Perhaps my favourite dessert from childhood, this British regional tart has been reimagined here without sugar or gluten, and with fresh fruit instead of jam. Undeniably modern and aligned to the way we eat now, while retaining its traditional Englishness, this tart is perfect for teatime

7 Remove the beans and paper, then return the pastry case (pie shell) to the oven and bake for 5 minutes more, then remove from the oven and set aside for about 5 minutes while you continue to prepare the frangipane.

8 Put the butter and coconut crystals in a mixing bowl. Cream together using an electric whisk on medium for about 2 minutes until fluffy, adding the almond extract in the last 30 seconds. Whisk in the eggs one by one. Fold in the flour mixture.

9 Pour the macerated raspberries into the tart, and top with the frangipane. Spread evenly with the silicone spatula, and return to the oven.

10 Bake for 20 minutes, then sprinkle the flaked almonds on the top. Return the tart to the oven and bake for 5–10 minutes more, until golden brown. Decorate with fresh raspberries before serving.

Mississippi Mud Pie was invented in the 1950s, and it was originally made from the highly processed ingredients that had recently become available in the USA. My version is just as fun as the original dessert, only much healthier! It still contains a lot of chocolate, but now that means using raw cacao, which is incredibly good for you. I've suggested using either granulated stevia or granulated monk fruit as a sweetener, as they are both made with a base of erythritol, so they act exactly the same in baked goods. If preferred, replace them with coconut crystals or maple sugar, but use double the amount.

Start preparing this pie at least a day ahead of serving, as the filling and the custard are both better if chilled in the refrigerator overnight.

Mississippi Mud Pie

SERVES 12

For the pastry:
15ml/1 tbsp vegetable oil, for greasing
225g/8oz/2 cups walnut pieces
115g/4oz/1 cup goji berries
50ml/2fl oz/¼ cup maple syrup
50g/2oz/¼ cup maple sugar

For the filling:
60ml/4 tbsp coconut oil
175g/6oz/1¾ cups raw cacao paste
6 eggs, separated
1.5ml/¼ tsp sea salt
50g/2oz/½ cup granulated stevia
   or monk fruit
45g/1¾oz/¼ cup agave powder

For the chocolate custard:
45ml/3 tbsp granulated stevia
   or monk fruit
50g/2oz/½ cup cacao powder
75ml/5 tbsp cornflour (cornstarch)
600ml/1 pint/2½ cups almond milk
45ml/3 tbsp coconut oil

For the cream topping:
300ml/½ pint/1¼ cups double (heavy)
   cream
cacao powder, for sprinkling

1 Preheat the oven to 180°C/350°F/Gas 4. Grease a 23cm/9in diameter springform cake tin or pan with oil.

2 To make the pastry, put the walnuts, goji berries, maple syrup and maple sugar in a food processor and process to form a sticky dough.

3 Press the dough into the cake tin, flattening it into the bottom and up the sides using the back of a spoon, leaving about 1cm/½in gap between the top of the crust and the top of the cake tin.

4 To make the filling, put the coconut oil and cacao paste in a heatproof bowl set over a pan of barely simmering water. Stir until combined.

5 Put the egg yolks, salt and the granulated stevia or monk fruit in a mixing bowl and beat with an electric whisk on high for about 5 minutes, until pale and have roughly doubled in volume. Wash and dry the beaters.

6 Put the egg whites in a separate clean, dry mixing bowl and beat with the electric whisk, starting on low and building up to high over a few minutes. Add the agave powder at the end, whisking until soft peaks form, but no more.

7 Gently fold the egg white mixture into the egg yolk mixture using a silicone spatula. Fold in the cacao and coconut oil mixture.

8 Pour the filling into the pastry, and bake for about 40 minutes until the batter has set, but is still wet enough to move a little when you shake the tin.

▶

Instead of using a processed whipped topping made out of nasty emulsifiers and hydrogenated fats, it's simply real dairy cream that's whipped: the most traditional creamy topping there is, with zero high-fructose corn syrup

9 Leave the pie to cool in the tin on a wire rack, where it will sink a little in the middle as it cools. When it has cooled to room temperature, chill in the refrigerator for at least 3 hours, or overnight.

10 To make the chocolate custard, put the granulated stevia or monk fruit in a pan with the cacao powder and cornflour and mix to combine. Slowly pour in the almond milk, whisking continuously with an electric whisk on low to make sure any lumps are crushed. Put the pan over a medium heat, and continue whisking as the liquid comes to a boil. Allow to boil for 30 seconds, then pour it into a bowl.

11 Add the coconut oil, and continue whisking on medium until the coconut oil has melted and combined into the custard.

12 Leave to cool for about 15 minutes and put the custard in the refrigerator to set for at least 3 hours, or overnight.

13 Once it has cooled and set, remove the custard from the refrigerator. Stir it with a spatula to break it up, then pour it over the cake and spread evenly, making sure to keep within the outer crust.

14 Put the cake back in the refrigerator for about half an hour, then remove the outer springform ring from the tin. Remove the bottom of the cake tin and put the cake on a stand.

15 To make the cream topping, pour the cream into a bowl and and beat with the electric whisk on high until it forms stiff peaks. Spread the cream over the top of the pie, sprinkle with cacao powder and serve immediately.

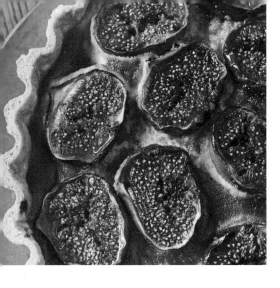

This pretty, caramelized tart showcases summer's fresh figs against a golden custard backdrop that's infused with cinnamon. Whether you use black figs or green, the natural sweetness of the fruit intensifies as they bake, and adds density to their texture.

I've suggested using granulated stevia in the pastry, but this is optional, and can be substituted with an equal amount of raw cane crystals or coconut crystals if preferred. Whichever sweetener you choose, the cinnamon and ground black pepper are wonderful accompaniments to the flavour of the figs.

Cinnamon Figgy Tart

SERVES 8

For the pastry:
250g/9oz/2 cups plain (all-purpose) flour, plus extra for dusting
30ml/2 tbsp granulated stevia (optional)
2.5ml/½ tsp baking powder
2.5ml/½ tsp sea salt
225g/8oz/1 cup unsalted butter, frozen and diced
50ml/2fl oz/¼ cup cold water

For the custard filling:
2 cinnamon sticks
175ml/6fl oz/¾ cup almond milk
175ml/6fl oz/¾ cup double (heavy) cream
1 egg, plus 1 egg yolk
25ml/1½ tbsp cornflour (cornstarch)
1.5ml/¼ tsp sea salt
45ml/3 tbsp granulated stevia
10ml/2 tsp vanilla extract
45ml/3 tbsp unsalted butter, softened

For the figs:
10 ripe figs, halved
30ml/2 tbsp almond oil
60ml/4 tbsp honey
sea salt and black pepper

1 To make the pastry, put all of the dry ingredients in a mixing bowl, then add the butter and either rub it in with your fingers, or pulse in a food processor to make pea-sized breadcrumbs. Rub or mix in the water.

2 Pour the mixture on to the counter and knead it briefly until it comes together as a dough, but no more. Form the dough into a disc and cover with clear film (plastic wrap). Chill for at least 1 hour, or overnight. When you're ready to make the rest of the tart, remove it from the refrigerator and bring to room temperature.

3 Grease a 30cm/12in diameter round flan tin or pan with sides that are about 2.5cm/1in deep.

4 Dust the counter with flour, then roll out the pastry to a circle of about 40cm/16in diameter, using a rolling pin.

5 Transfer the pastry into the tin with the rolling pin, then press it gently into the bottom and up the sides. Cut away excess pastry, leaving a generous amount in expectation of the pastry shrinking while it bakes. Freeze for at least 1 hour, or overnight.

6 To make the filling, put the cinnamon sticks in a pan with the almond milk and cream. Gently warm over a low heat, uncovered.

7 Put the egg, the additional yolk, cornflour, salt, stevia and vanilla in a bowl and beat with a hand whisk or an electric whisk on low.

8 Raise the heat on the pan to medium and slowly bring the milk to a boil, then set aside for 10 minutes to cool slightly. Add 15ml/1 tbsp of the egg mixture at a time and whisk, incorporating after each addition.

▶

This pretty, caramelized tart showcases summer's fresh figs against a golden custard backdrop that's infused with cinnamon. Whether you use black figs or green, the fruits get denser and sweeter as they bake

9 Put the pan back over a medium heat and continue whisking on low as the custard comes to a boil. Allow to boil for about 2 minutes, still whisking, until thick. Remove the cinnamon sticks, then whisk in the butter.

10 Heat the oven to 180°C/350°F/ Gas 4. Line the top of the pastry with a circle of baking parchment. Weigh it down with a few dry beans and bake for 30 minutes, then remove the beans and return to the oven for another 20 minutes until very brown. Allow the pastry to cool for about half an hour.

11 While the pastry is cooling, lay the figs cut side up on a plate and drizzle them with almond oil and honey. Season with ground sea salt and black pepper and set aside for about 1 hour while the pastry is cooling.

12 Pour the custard filling into the pastry case or pie shell, and distribute it evenly with a palette knife. Arrange the figs evenly on top of the tart, cut sides up. Bake for 1½ hours, until the custard has set and the figs are caramelized. Allow to cool in the tin and serve at room temperature.

COOK'S TIP
The custard filling and the pastry are sweetened with granulated stevia, but this can be replaced with coconut sugar, if preferred. Replace the stated amount of stevia with 75ml/5 tbsp coconut sugar for the custard filling, and 60ml/4 tbsp coconut sugar for the pastry. The almond oil for the figs can be replaced with melted coconut oil or butter, if preferred.

Perhaps more American than any other dessert, pumpkin pie is the showpiece of the Thanksgiving dinner table. This pie can be made with any variety of pumpkin, and I also love making it with butternut squash. It's impossible to judge the amount of uncooked pumpkin that will provide 450g/1lb of cooked pumpkin, so cook more than you need, then weigh the amount that is required for this recipe. Alternatively, use canned pumpkin, but it's just not as good!

The pastry is generously thick and slightly sweetened with honey, and the top is layered with very pretty pastry leaves. Try decorating this pie with any pastry shape that can be cut with a cookie cutter, from plain circles to stars or even gingerbread men!

Pumpkin Pie

SERVES 8

For the purée:
1 large piece of pumpkin, or 1 butternut squash, halved and deseeded
50ml/2fl oz/¼ cup sunflower oil
250ml/8fl oz/1 cup water

For the pastry:
15ml/1 tbsp butter at room temperature, for greasing
30ml/2 tbsp honey
45ml/3 tbsp warm water
250g/9oz/2 cups plain (all-purpose) flour, plus extra for dusting
2.5ml/½ tsp sea salt
175g/6oz/¾ cup unsalted butter, frozen

For the filling:
150ml/5fl oz/⅔ cup honey
3 eggs, lightly beaten
30ml/2 tbsp cornflour (cornstarch)
10ml/2 tsp ground cinnamon
5ml/1 tsp ground ginger

1.5ml/¼ tsp sea salt
150ml/5fl oz/⅔ cup double (heavy) cream

1 Preheat the oven to 180°C/350°F/Gas 4.

2 Rub the surface of the pumpkin or squash with oil, then place the piece or halves cut-side down in an oiled roasting pan. Pour the water into the pan and roast for 1½ hours, or until tender enough to pierce easily with a sharp knife. Remove from the oven and set aside until still warm but cool enough to handle, then scrape the flesh away from the skin.

3 Put 450g/1lb/2 cups of the pumpkin flesh in a blender and process to a purée. Pour the purée into a large sieve or strainer lined with muslin or cheesecloth suspended over a mixing bowl and leave to drain for 2 hours.

4 When the purée is ready, lightly grease a 23cm/9in pie dish with butter and preheat the oven to 180°C/350°F/Gas 4.

5 To make the pastry, put the honey and water in a cup and mix until combined, then put it in the freezer to chill until needed.

6 Sift the flour and salt into a mixing bowl. Using a box grater, coarsely grate the frozen butter into the bowl, dipping the block of butter in flour now and then to keep it from sticking to the grater.

7 Drizzle about half the honey water into the bowl and mix with your fingertips until a dough starts to form. Add more liquid a little at a time, if needed, until the dough is stretchy without being wet.

▶

Pumpkins originated in the Americas, and have become associated with fairies and magical tales. Heirloom pumpkins come in a huge variety of shapes, sizes and colours, including French heirloom varieties in the palest of pastel whites and greens, and American giants in deepest orange

8 Dust the counter and a rolling pin with flour, and roll out the dough until it's about 1cm/½in thick. Gently fold it in half, and transfer the pastry to the pie dish using the rolling pin. Crimp the edges around the top of the dish using your fingers. Trim the excess pastry with a sharp knife, then re-roll the scraps into a ball. Flour the counter well, and roll out the pastry again, until it's about 1cm/½in thick.

9 Stamp out leaves using a cookie cutter, or cut them out by hand with a sharp knife and continue combining scraps, re-rolling and cutting until all the pastry has been used up.

10 To make the filling, put the drained pumpkin purée in a large bowl and mix in the honey, eggs, cornflour, spices, salt and cream.

11 Pour the filling into the pastry case or pie shell, then layer the pastry leaves over the top, around the outer circumference of the pie so that they overlap from the edge towards the centre. Keep layering the pastry leaves from the outer edges towards the middle until you run out of leaves. Leave a circle of at least 6cm/2½in clear of pastry leaves in the middle of the pie.

12 Bake the pie in the preheated oven for about 1¼ hours until the pastry is golden. The filling should still be fluid enough to wobble when you shake the pie. Leave the pie to cool in the dish, and serve at room temperature.

Inspired by an old blues singer in Greenwich Village, this pie will make your loved ones sing too! Rye flour makes a hearty golden pastry, which makes a beautiful contrast to the dark red cherry juices that ooze out of this pie, dappling the surface with sticky pools of cherry toffee.

Pitting cherries is simple and it only takes a few minutes to pit enough to make this sensual summer pie. I simply use a piping (icing) nozzle and push the fruit on to it, one by one. Designate this task to older children if you want, or enjoy doing it while listening to the radio on a summer's afternoon.

Cherry Pie

SERVES 8

For the pastry:
200g/7oz/1½ cups rye flour
200g/7oz/1½ cups plain (all-purpose) flour, plus extra for dusting
15ml/1 tbsp raw cane crystals
0.6ml/⅛ tsp sea salt
225g/8oz/2 sticks cold, unsalted butter
120ml/4fl oz/½ cup ice-cold water
2.5ml/½ tsp almond extract

For the filling:
450g/1lb/6 cups ripe dark red cherries, stoned (pitted) and stems removed
30ml/2 tbsp rye flour
150g/5oz/1 cup raw cane crystals
50g/2oz/⅓ cup ground almonds

For the glaze:
15ml/1 tbsp milk
2.5ml/½ tsp raw cane crystals

1 To make the pastry, sift the flours into a large mixing bowl. Mix in the raw cane crystals and salt. Dice the butter into roughly 1cm/½in cubes. Mix the water with the almond extract in a cup.

2 Rub the butter into the flour very lightly and quickly with your fingertips to make a texture of coarse breadcrumbs, with some big pea-sized bits of butter still visible. Add 100ml/3½fl oz/scant ½ cup of the almond water a little at a time, mixing it in gently with your fingers. Keep adding water tablespoon by tablespoon until the dough is wet enough to hold together in a ball.

3 Divide the dough into two equal discs and cover with clear film (plastic wrap). Chill for at least 30 minutes, but preferably overnight. The pastry dough can be stored in the freezer at this stage for up to 2 weeks.

▶

Rye flour makes a hearty golden pastry, which is a beautiful contrast to the dark red cherry juices that ooze out of this pie, dappling the surface with sticky pools of cherry toffee

4 Heat the oven to 220°C/425°F/Gas 7. Grease a 23cm/9in diameter pie dish with butter.

5 To make the filling, put the cherries in a large non-reactive bowl with the flour and cane crystals, and set aside.

6 Dust the counter and a rolling pin with rye flour, then roll out one disc of pastry into a circle of about 30cm/12in diameter and 3mm/⅛in thick, using the rolling pin.

7 Fold the pastry in half gently, then transfer it to the pie dish with the rolling pin. Press the sides gently to fill the corners and cut away any excess pastry with a knife.

8 Sprinkle the ground almonds inside the bottom of the pie, then pour in the cherry mixture and spread evenly.

9 Remove the second pastry disc from the refrigerator and roll it out to a circle of about 30cm/12in diameter and 3mm/⅛in thick. Transfer the pastry to the top of the pie using the rolling pin, and press down the edges of the pie to seal the pastry. Cut away any excess pastry, re-roll and cut into leaf-shaped decorations, using a sharp knife.

10 Top the pie with pastry leaves and brush with the milk. Sprinkle with raw cane crystals and bake in the preheated oven for 15 minutes, then reduce the heat to 190°C/375°F/Gas 5.

11 Bake for about 25 minutes, then check if it is deep golden brown. Bake for 15–20 minutes more, then remove from the oven. Set aside for 5 minutes before serving warm, or cool completely and then serve cold.

RUSTIC GALETTE

To transform this classic pie into a rustic galette, grease and line a baking sheet (with sides) with baking parchment. Roll out one disc of pastry to about 30cm/12in, and lay it on top of the paper. Sprinkle with ground almonds and spread over the cherry mixture, leaving a 4–5cm/1½–2in margin around the sides, then roughly fold up the sides to form a rim. Brush with the milk and sprinkle over the raw cane crystals. Bake the galette as described above.

When cooked, carefully slide the galette off the paper and allow to cool on a wire crack. It will look messy, with spilled juice leaving sticky trails over the edges, but that's the fun! Serve cold with clotted cream.

Special Occasion Cakes

Birthday cakes, Christmas cakes, wedding cakes and simple tea cakes... if you need a special occasion cake without the sugar, this is the place to find it! Need it no-sugar and gluten-free too? Try a classic Flourless Chocolate Roll. After something squishy and nostalgic? Go for the Lemon Drizzle Loaf Cake. And, if you're after a show-stopper, look no further than my Victoria Sponge Supreme.

No-sugar cakes don't have to be sensible and boring. In this chapter, you'll discover how to bake the most beautiful and luxurious cakes that will make the perfect centrepiece for any occasion

Sugar-free, gluten-free and dairy-free, this rich and extremely moist cake can be eaten straight from the oven as a hot dessert, or served cold, in which case the consistency improves after a few days. It's sweetened primarily with sweet potatoes grated into the cake. I've also added dried figs, which are essential to include in any Christmas cake. It's what makes it Christmassy. Start preparing this festive treat a day ahead of serving, as the figs and almonds need to soak in the orange purée overnight. Serve with custard, whipped cream or no-sugar vanilla ice cream.

Christmas Fruit and Nut Cake

SERVES 12
1 navel orange, unpeeled and cut into pieces
75g/3oz/½ cup chopped dried figs
115g/4oz/1 cup slivered almonds
15ml/1 tbsp vegetable oil or butter, for greasing
90g/3oz/1½ cups oats
3 eggs, loosely beaten
250g/9oz/2 cups grated sweet potatoes
75g/3oz/1 cup desiccated (dried unsweetened shredded) coconut
50g/2oz/½ cup ground almonds
175ml/6fl oz/¾ cup coconut oil
115g/4oz/½ cup coconut crystals
15ml/1 tbsp bicarbonate of soda (baking soda)
2.5ml/½ tsp sea salt
5ml/1 tsp ground cinnamon
5ml/1 tsp ground ginger
2.5ml/½ tsp ground nutmeg
2.5ml/½ tsp ground cloves

1 Put the orange pieces in a blender and blend to a purée. Mix half of the blended orange with the figs and half with the almonds, and leave to soak overnight in the refrigerator.

2 Preheat the oven to 180°C/350°F/ Gas 4. Grease a 23cm/9in diameter round springform cake tin or pan with oil or butter.

3 Put the oats in a food processor and pulse for about 30 seconds to pulverize.

4 Put the eggs in a large mixing bowl. Add all the other ingredients, and stir to combine.

5 Pour the batter into the cake tin, and bake for 40–50 minutes, until a skewer inserted into the middle comes out clean.

6 Leave to cool in the tin for 10 minutes before removing the springform sides, then serve warm or leave to cool on a wire rack if serving cold.

Sugar-free, gluten-free and dairy-free, this rich, moist cake can be eaten straight from the oven as a hot dessert, or served cold as it improves after a few days. It's delicious served with custard, whipped cream or vanilla ice cream

Possibly the greatest of all birthday cakes, I've upgraded and modernized this much-loved classic into a no-sugar, gluten-free, super-fun recipe! Four cakes, layered one on top of the other, are presented here as a towering centrepiece fit for any party. A trusted birthday cake. A tea party extravaganza. A cake for weddings, anniversaries, baby showers, or any special occasion.

Although I am happy to eat foods that contain gluten, the benefit of baking gluten-free cakes for a party or a gathering is that everybody will be able to share a piece. My trick to keep this gluten-free recipe fluffy is to make the batter a little runnier than if you were making it with plain (all-purpose) flour. Why not try my own gluten-free flour recipe below?

Victoria Sponge Supreme

SERVES 12

For the filling:
1kg/2¼lb/2 quarts fresh strawberries, hulled and quartered
juice of ½ lemon
50ml/2fl oz/¼ cup raw agave syrup
500ml/1 pint/2 cups coconut cream, or dairy whipping cream if preferred, chilled in the refrigerator

For the cakes:
450g/1lb/4 sticks butter
275g/10oz/2 cups coconut sugar
20ml/4 tsp vanilla extract
6 eggs
450g/1lb/4 cups gluten-free flour mix
15ml/3 tsp baking powder
500ml/17fl oz/generous 2 cups almond milk, or whole dairy milk
agave powder, for sprinkling (optional)
fresh flowers, to decorate (optional)

1 To make the filling, put the strawberries in a non-reactive bowl. Put the lemon juice in a cup and mix in the agave syrup. Pour it over the strawberries. Cover with clear film (plastic wrap), and macerate in the refrigerator for at least 4 hours, or overnight.

2 To make the cakes, preheat the oven to 180°C/350°F/Gas 4. Lightly grease two non-stick 23cm/9in diameter round 5cm/2in deep cake tins or pans.

3 Cream 225g/8oz/2 sticks of the butter, 150g/5oz/1 cup of the coconut sugar, and 10ml/2 tsp of the vanilla in a mixing bowl with a wooden spoon. One by one, mix in 3 of the eggs.

4 Sift in 225g/8oz/2 cups of the flour and 7.5ml/1½ tsp of the baking powder, and stir. Little by little, add 250ml/8fl oz/1 cup of the almond milk.

5 Pour the batter equally into the cake tins and bake for about 45 minutes, until a skewer inserted into the middle comes out clean.

6 Turn the cakes out onto a wire rack and set aside to cool. Repeat these steps to use up the rest of the cake ingredients and bake two more cakes, so there are a total of four. ▶

GLUTEN-FREE FLOUR
MAKES 1KG/2¼LB

450g/1lb/2¾ cups brown rice flour
325g/11½oz/2 cups potato starch
325g/11½oz/2 cups oat flour

Sift all the ingredients together in a mixing bowl and store in a clean, dry, airtight container in the refrigerator for freshness.

Fresh strawberries are macerated, then piled on top of a whipped coconut cream layer, oozing out of the sides in a fairytale cake way. Any little birthday princess will be satisfied by this beauty. As the strawberries are best served after soaking overnight, prepare the strawberries before you bake the cakes.

8 Put one of the cakes onto a serving plate or a tiered cake stand. Spread a third of the cream on top of the cake using a silicone spatula, or a palette knife. Spread a quarter of the strawberries on top. Put the second cake on top to make a sandwich.

9 Spread an equal amount of the whipped cream on top of the second cake evenly. Top with an equal amount of strawberries. Put the third cake on top, and spread over the remaining cream. Add an equal amount of the strawberries. Top the fourth cake and finish with the remaining strawberries.

7 When all four cakes have been baked, cooled, and are ready to be assembled, remove the coconut or dairy cream from the refrigerator. Whisk until it is thick and stiff peaks form, using an electric whisk or hand whisk.

10 Leave for about 1 hour, so that the cake has a little time to absorb some of the cream and strawberry juices and set. Dust the cake with agave powder and decorate with fresh flowers before serving, if liked.

This is a very pretty pink cake piled with macerated strawberries. The colour comes from all natural, vegetarian unrefined sources, including beetroot, strawberries and a superfood called yum berry powder. Yum berries are brightly coloured red berries full of antioxidants. Not only is this cake sugar-free, it's incredibly moist and utterly delicious. And more importantly, unlike most red velvet cakes, it doesn't contain any store-bought food colourings made from petrochemicals or insects!

Cut a slice to reveal a soft brown velvety sponge that's dappled with little flecks of red. It's moist and indulgent, and will appeal to adults and children alike when served as a very special birthday cake.

Pink Velvet Cake

SERVES 16

For the cakes:
5 medium beetroot (beets), unpeeled and cut into chunks
200g/7oz/2 cups ground almonds
250g/9oz/2 cups plain (all-purpose) flour
50g/2oz/½ cup yum berry powder
60ml/4 tbsp raw cacao powder
30ml/2 tbsp baking powder
5ml/1 tsp sea salt
250ml/8fl oz/1 cup buttermilk
10ml/2 tsp apple cider vinegar
10ml/2 tsp vanilla extract
225g/8oz/1 cup unsalted butter, at room temperature
450g/1lb/3 cups erythritol crystals
4 eggs

For the topping:
2kg/4½lb/2 quarts fresh strawberries, hulled and quartered
60ml/4 tbsp barley malt syrup

For the frosting:
115g/4oz/½ cup unsalted butter, at room temperature
450g/1lb/2 cups cream cheese
15ml/1 tbsp vanilla extract
5ml/1 tsp apple cider vinegar
250ml/8fl oz/1 cup barley malt syrup
fresh pink rose petals, to decorate

1 To make the cakes, put the beetroot in a blender, and add enough cold water to blend into juice and pulp. Sink a measuring jug or cup into the blended juice and pulp mixture to catch the juice in it. Retain the pulp and store in the refrigerator until you are ready to make the frosting.

2 Put the ground almonds in a bowl with 250ml/8fl oz/1 cup of the beetroot juice and set aside to soak for at least half an hour, or overnight.

3 To make the topping, put the strawberries in a bowl. Mix in the barley malt syrup and leave to macerate for at least 1 hour, or overnight.

4 Preheat the oven to 180°C/350°F/ Gas 4 and oil four 23cm/9in diameter round cake tins or pans.

5 To continue making the cakes, sift the flour, yum berry powder, cacao, baking powder and salt into a bowl. In a separate small bowl, mix together the buttermilk, vinegar and vanilla.

6 Cream the butter with the erythritol crystals in a mixing bowl, using the back of a spoon, until combined, then continue to cream with an electric whisk on high for about 3 minutes, until very creamy. Add the eggs one by one, whisking each on medium for 1 minute to combine.

▶

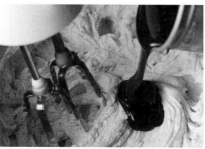

Artificial pink and red food colourings are made from chemical ingredients that can be traced back to crude oil. Red velvet cake relies on red food colouring being added, because that's how the sponge cake inside gets its redness. This recipe avoids the pitfalls of choosing between artificial or natural red food colouring by using fresh ingredients to add vibrant shades of pink and red.

7 Add the almond and beetroot mixture and whisk for about 30 seconds on high. Add about a quarter of the flour mixture, and whisk again for about 30 seconds. Add about a quarter of the buttermilk mixture, and whisk for about 30 seconds, until just combined. Little by little, add the rest of the flour mixture and the buttermilk mixture, working quickly so that they are combined, but aren't left to stand too long.

8 Pour the batter equally into the cake tins, and bake for 25–30 minutes, or until a skewer inserted into the middle comes out clean. Allow to cool in the tins on a wire rack for about 15 minutes, then turn them out to cool completely on the rack.

9 To make the frosting, cream the butter with the cream cheese in a large bowl with an electric whisk. Add the vanilla, vinegar and barley malt syrup and continue whisking until smooth.

10 Add 60ml/4 tbsp of the beetroot pulp to the frosting mixture along with 50ml/2fl oz/¼ cup of the soaking liquid from the strawberries. Whisk to combine.

11 Put one cake on a platter or stand, and spread about a fifth of the frosting mixture evenly on top, using a palette knife. Put the second cake on top to make a sandwich, and spread with more of the frosting. Keep going until all four cakes have been assembled and spread with the pink frosting.

12 Complete the cake by covering the top and sides with frosting. Pile the strawberry pieces onto the top of the cake and arrange fresh pink rose petals around the base of the platter to decorate.

COOK'S TIP:
If you're unable to find yum berry powder, replace it with plain (all-purpose) flour.

This is my adaptation of a traditional Moroccan recipe that's become one of my favourites. It never fails to be enjoyed by my guests, whether they're on a gluten-free diet, or if they love eating the most indulgent things. I've yet to meet someone who hasn't asked for a second slice! Also, the kitchen smells incredible as the oranges cook, and just gets better as the cake bakes.

This is not an inexpensive cake, as it contains a lot of nuts and coconut sugar, and it's rich for that reason, too. It's not an everyday dessert, but is perfect for a special occasion. If you would like to make your own vegan, sugar-free chocolate sauce, use the recipe for Raw Vegan Chocolates on page 183 but keep the chocolate warm instead of chilling to solidify.

Orange and Almond Cake

SERVES 12

3 medium oranges or 2 large
   navel oranges
5ml/1 tsp coconut oil, for greasing
6 eggs
450g/1lb/2¼ cups coconut sugar
500g/1¼lb/5½ cups ground almonds
7.5ml/1½ tsp baking powder
sugar-free chocolate sauce,
   to serve (optional)

1 Bring a large pan of water to the boil over a high heat. Add the whole oranges, put the lid on the pan, reduce the heat and simmer for 30 minutes. Remove the oranges from the water with a slotted spoon and discard the cooking water. Leave the fruit to cool.

2 Preheat the oven to 180°C/350°F/ Gas 4. Oil a 23cm/9in diameter round springform cake tin or pan with the coconut oil.

3 When the oranges are cool enough to handle easily, cut them in half along their circumferences. Remove the seeds. Transfer them to a blender, and process for about 20 seconds on high until puréed.

4 Put the eggs in a large mixing bowl and add the coconut sugar. Gently beat with a fork to combine, then add the orange purée and mix it in with a large spoon or a silicone spatula. Add the ground almonds and baking powder and fold in the dry ingredients, working quickly.

5 Pour the batter into the cake tin, and roughly even out the surface. Bake for about 50 minutes, until a skewer inserted into the middle comes out clean. If it's cooked a little longer, the outside may be darker in colour, but it will have a richer flavour.

6 Leave the cake in the tin to cool completely. Remove the sides from the cake tin and put it on a serving plate. Serve on its own, or with chocolate sauce, if liked.

It never fails to be enjoyed by my guests, whether they're on a gluten-free diet or if they love eating the most indulgent things. I've yet to meet someone who hasn't asked for a second slice!

This cake is a great bridge between generations, it can just as easily be served as a birthday cake for children, or a dinner party finale for your friends. It's gluten-free as well as no-sugar, but I've used old-fashioned dairy to create the chocolate cream layer. If you'd like to replace the filling with something non-dairy, the rest of the cake can be made vegan by using a high-quality vegan yogurt such as almond yogurt.

I've suggested using two 25cm/10in springform cake tins or pans, but if you only have 23cm/9in, they'll work perfectly well. Just make sure they are well-oiled and all will be wonderful.

Vanilla and Chocolate Layer Cake

SERVES 16

For the cakes:
550ml/18fl oz/2½ cups Greek (US strained plain) yogurt
150ml/¼ pint/⅔ cup olive oil, plus extra for greasing
200g/7oz/1½ cups coconut crystals
15–20ml/3–4 tsp vanilla extract, to taste
5 eggs
225g/8oz/2 cups brown rice flour
90g/3½oz/¾ cup oat flour
125g/4¼oz/generous 1 cup potato starch
20ml/4 tsp baking powder
5ml/1 tsp sea salt

For the chocolate cream:
225g/8oz/1 cup unsalted butter, at room temperature
450g/1lb/2 cups cream cheese, at room temperature
200g/7oz/1½ cups agave powder
20g/¾oz/¼ cup cacao powder
30–60ml/2–4 tbsp agave syrup, to taste

1 Preheat the oven to 180°C/350°F/ Gas 4. Grease two 25cm/10in diameter round springform baking tins or pans with oil.

2 To make the cakes, put the yogurt, oil, coconut crystals and vanilla in a mixing bowl. Using an electric whisk on low, add the eggs one by one, incorporating each one before adding the next. Add the rest of the ingredients and stir gently with a wooden spoon to combine.

3 Pour half the batter into each of the cake tins, and smooth with a silicone spatula. Bake for 45 minutes, until golden brown and the edges are slightly separated from the tins.

4 Remove the cakes from the oven and allow to cool in the tins for about 15 minutes, then remove the springform sides and leave to cool on a wire rack.

5 When they are completely cool, make the chocolate cream. Put all of the ingredients into a large bowl and cream together for about 2 minutes, using an electric whisk on medium.

6 Put one of the cakes on a large plate or a cake stand. Spread half the chocolate cream evenly over the top. Carefully put the second cake on top, to create a sandwich. Spread the top with the remaining chocolate cream, using a silicone spatula to create a swirl to decorate, then serve.

Make sure the batter bakes evenly and the cakes will stack a little more firmly

Carrot cake was hugely popular in the 1970s health movement because it contained less sugar than other popular cakes of that era. However, this seems to have been lost over time as most carrot cake today contains a lot of refined sugar, and often high-fructose corn syrup too.

For this recipe, I've removed the refined sugars by adding fresh and dried fruit. In addition, there's a little coconut sugar to make the texture sticky, and the spices also boost the natural sweetness. I've also added yacon powder, but if you can't find it, it's fine to use maple sugar instead. Truly a wonderful sugar-free cake that you can rely on, it is not only no-sugar but low in lactose and gluten too! Start preparing this cake the day before serving.

Carrot and Apple Cake

SERVES 12

For the cake:
rind and juice of ½ medium orange
115g/4oz/¾ cup sultanas (golden raisins)
115g/4oz/¾ cup chopped walnuts
2 eggs
185g/6½oz/1½ cups grated carrots
75g/3oz/¾ cup grated apples
185g/6½oz/1½ cups spelt flour
175ml/6fl oz/¾ cup coconut oil
150g/5oz/¾ cup coconut sugar
25g/1oz/¼ cup yacon powder or maple sugar
10ml/2 tsp bicarbonate of soda (baking soda)
5ml/1 tsp sea salt
10ml/2 tsp ground cinnamon
2.5ml/½ tsp ground nutmeg
2.5ml/½ tsp ground ginger

For the frosting:
115g/4oz/½ cup unsalted butter
225g/8oz/1 cup chévre (goat's cheese)
200g/7oz/1 cup maple sugar
5ml/1 tsp vanilla extract (optional)
fresh flowers, to decorate (optional)

1 Put the orange juice and rind in a small bowl and add the sultanas. In another small bowl, cover the walnuts with water. Put both bowls in the refrigerator, and leave to soak overnight.

2 The next day, preheat the oven to 180°C/350°F/Gas 4, and grease two 23cm/9in round cake tins or pans with oil.

3 Beat the eggs in a large mixing bowl. Drain the nuts, discarding the soaking water, and add to the bowl. Add the sultanas, orange juice and rind, and all the other ingredients. Mix to combine, then pour the batter into the tins or pans.

4 Bake for 40–50 minutes, until a skewer inserted into the middle comes out clean. Leave to cool in the tins for about 15 minutes.

5 Turn out the cakes onto a large serving platter, cover and leave to cool completely.

6 To make the frosting, cream the butter and chévre together in a bowl, using a fork. Add the maple sugar and vanilla, if using, and continue to cream. When the cakes are ready to serve, spread the top of one cake with half the frosting using a spatula. Top with the second cake and spread over the remaining frosting in an even layer. Decorate with fresh flowers before serving, if liked.

Moist and intensely chocolatey, this sophisticated version of a Swiss roll is perfect at any time of year. Served in summer, it can be garnished with fresh fruit, and at Christmas it becomes a Yule log.

My mother gave me the original recipe, which I adored as a child. It's related to a soufflé, so it involves a lot of eggs. If you follow the instructions carefully, this cake will work, but make sure to keep an eye on it as it bakes, as the edges are susceptible to burning due to the thin depth of the sponge before it's rolled.

Flourless Chocolate Roll

SERVES 12

25g/1oz/¼ cup coconut oil, melted, plus extra for greasing
40g/1½oz/¼ cup raw cacao powder
40g/1½oz/¼ cup Peruvian carob or mesquite powder
6 eggs, at room temperature
1.5ml/¼ tsp cream of tartar
150g/5oz/1 cup coconut sugar
ground cinnamon, to taste
30ml/2 tbsp agave powder, for dusting
300ml/½ pint/1½ cups whipping cream

1 Preheat the oven to 190°C/375°F/Gas 5. Lightly grease a 33cm x 23cm/13in x 9in Swiss roll (jelly roll) tin or pan with oil, then line the base and sides with baking parchment.

2 Sift the cacao and mesquite powder into a large bowl, then pour in the coconut oil. Mix thoroughly with a metal spoon and set aside.

3 Separate the eggs. Collect the whites in a large glass bowl, and the yolks in a small bowl. Add the cream of tartar to the whites.

4 Add the egg yolks to the cacao mixture, then stir in the coconut sugar and set aside.

5 Beat the egg whites to form stiff peaks, but no more, using an electric whisk on high. Set aside.

6 Beat the egg yolk and cacao mixture for 2–3 minutes, until creamy. The mixture will leave thick trails when the whisk is lifted.

7 Gently stir about 30ml/2 tbsp of the egg whites into the mixture, then carefully fold the remaining egg whites into the chocolate with a metal spoon, retaining as much of the air as possible.

8 Pour the batter into the tin, then gently tilt the tin from side to side until the batter is level. Bake in the preheated oven for 18–20 minutes until risen and firm to the touch. Remove from the oven, and leave in the tin to cool.

9 When the cake is cool, wash and dry the beaters, then pour the cream into a clean bowl, and whisk on high until thick. Spread the cream over the cake using a metal spoon, leaving a 2.5cm/1in border.

10 Starting with one of the shorter edges, roll the cake, using the baking parchment. Peel the paper away as the cake rolls from one side of the tin to the other. Put the finished roll on a serving platter, and dust with agave powder, before serving.

This is my new spin on an old classic, and to be honest... it's possibly even yummier than the sugary version! Gluten-free because of the ground almonds and oat flour, it is pleasantly sticky and light as a feather, yet one of the moistest cakes you can imagine. It's the perfect birthday cake to bake for a friend, or to pack for a picnic treat by the sea, as the salty air complements the lemony flavour in a most delightful way.

Lemon Drizzle Loaf Cake

SERVES 8

grated rind and juice of 2 medium
  lemons
175g/6oz/¾ cup unsalted butter,
  softened, plus extra for greasing
225g/8oz/generous 1 cup coconut sugar
3 eggs
100g/3¾oz/scant 1 cup oat flour
15ml/1 tbsp baking powder
75g/3oz/¾ cup ground almonds
150ml/¼ pint/⅔ cup almond milk or
  Greek (US strained plain) yogurt
thin strips of lemon rind, to decorate

The perfect birthday cake to bake for a friend, or to pack for a picnic by the sea

1 Preheat the oven to 180°C/350°F/Gas 4. Grease a 900g/2lb loaf tin or pan, and line it with baking parchment.

2 Put half the lemon rind in a large mixing bowl. Add the butter and cream together with 175g/6oz/scant 1 cup of the coconut sugar.

3 Add 1 egg to the butter mixture, and 5ml/1 tsp of the flour, and beat on high with an electric whisk to combine. Repeat for each of the eggs, adding a teaspoon of flour with each.

4 Sift the remaining flour, baking powder and ground almonds into the bowl. Fold the dry ingredients into the creamed butter, working quickly, using a spatula. Mix in the almond milk or yogurt little by little until just thin enough to fall off the spoon, but no more. It's unlikely you'll need all of the liquid.

5 Spoon the batter into the loaf tin, and bake in the preheated oven for 40–55 minutes.

6 Meanwhile, mix the lemon juice and remaining rind with the remaining coconut sugar and set aside to dissolve.

7 Remove the cake from the oven. It's done when a skewer inserted into the middle comes out clean. As soon as the cake has come out of the oven, prick the surface of the hot cake with a fork to pepper it with holes.

8 Pour the lemon juice mixture over the cake as evenly as possible, allowing it to sink in before pouring more on. The cake will be able to absorb all of it. Leave to cool inside the tin, then lift out of the tin by the edges of the paper and decorate with thin strips of lemon rind.

Sugar-free, vegan, gluten-free, heart-healthy, and full of fibre, this cakey bread is best served at teatime in toasted, buttered slices. I love it with really good organic butter, but it's also luscious spread with almond butter and whipped honey, or with a thin layer of hardened coconut oil.

Soaking the sultanas in tea keeps them juicy as they bake. Replace the black tea with herbal tea if preferred. Hibiscus or fruit teas are fragrant alternatives, or simply soak the sultanas in warm water. They have a wonderful flavour and just need to be plumped up a bit, which plain warm water does very nicely.

Oat Fruit Bread

SERVES 8

115g/4oz/1 cup sultanas (golden raisins)
120ml/4fl oz /½ cup hot English Breakfast tea
12 raw cashews
15ml/1 tbsp coconut oil, plus extra for greasing
3 ripe bananas, halved lengthways
juice of ½ lemon
45ml/3 tbsp apple juice
120ml/4fl oz/½ cup barley malt syrup
225g/8oz/2½ cups rolled oats
15ml/1 tbsp bicarbonate of soda (baking soda)
2.5ml/½ tsp sea salt
5ml/1 tsp ground cinnamon
5ml/1 tsp ground ginger
2.5ml/½ tsp ground nutmeg

1 Put the sultanas in a bowl and cover with the tea. Put the cashews in a cup and cover with warm water. Set aside to soak, overnight if possible.

2 Preheat the oven to 180°C/350°F/ Gas 4. Lightly oil a 23cm x 13cm/ 9in x 5in loaf tin or pan, and line with baking parchment.

3 Melt the coconut oil in a frying pan over a medium heat and fry the bananas for 1–2 minutes. Turn them over, and fry the other side for 1–2 minutes. Remove the frying pan from the heat, and set it aside so the bananas continue to gently steam in the residual heat.

4 Put the juices in a blender. Discard the soaking water from the cashews. Add the cashews, caramelized bananas and any liquid that's collected in the frying pan, and the barley malt syrup. Blend on high for 20–30 seconds, until combined, then pour the banana mixture into a large mixing bowl.

5 In a food processor, pulverize the oats, bicarbonate of soda, salt and spices for 30 seconds–1 minute, until they have become the consistency of flour.

6 Stir the dry ingredients into the wet ingredients. Add the sultanas and their soaking juices to the bowl. Combine quickly with a spatula or a spoon. Pour the batter into the loaf tin and quickly even the top.

7 Bake for about 35–40 minutes, until a skewer inserted into the middle comes out clean. Lift the loaf out of the tin using the baking parchment, and set aside to cool completely on a wire rack. Cut into slices and spread with butter to serve.

Cupcakes, Slices and Scones

Bring out the bunting! Lay out your tiered plates and silver forks. Spare not your bone china, chintz or paper doilies – it's teatime, and we have little cakes! Be they muffins, cupcakes, brownies or magdalenas these dainty delights are all sweet enough to serve with a pot of tea – and all are made with absolutely no sugar!

These dainty bites will be leaving crumbs around your home in the upcoming months. They are so more-ish that you'll find yourself baking a batch even for the most casual moments!

Is there anything better than sugar-free, vegan chocolate cupcakes? This recipe is sweetened primarily with bananas and it avoids eggs by using ground flax seeds instead. Make sure you use extremely ripe bananas that are blackened on their skins and very soft. This will ensure the cupcakes are moist and luscious.

Carob has acquired a reputation in recent years for not being delicious, but that's not true! It's a wonderful ingredient to use alongside cacao. It gently sweetens the cacao to produce a smoother, more chocolatey flavour. In addition, the carob also supports the bananas in gently sweetening the cupcakes without the need for sugar. The brown rice malt syrup and coconut milk help sweeten them too, and provide a good balance of moisture. Serve at any time of day.

Chocolate Banana Cupcakes

MAKES 10–12
4 large, ripe bananas
150ml/¼ pint/⅔ cup sunflower oil
90ml/6 tbsp brown rice malt syrup
90ml/6 tbsp coconut milk
10ml/2 tsp vanilla extract
75g/3oz/½ cup cacao powder
75g/3oz/½ cup carob powder
115g/4oz/1 cup plain (all-purpose)
    wholemeal (whole-wheat) flour
25g/1oz/¼ cup ground almonds
45ml/3 tbsp ground flax seeds
15ml/1 tbsp bicarbonate of soda
    (baking soda)
2.5ml/½ tsp ground cinnamon
2.5ml/½ tsp sea salt

1 Preheat the oven to 180°C/350°F/ Gas 4. Line a cupcake tin or pan with cupcake cases or papers.

2 Mash the bananas in a medium bowl. Add the oil, brown rice malt syrup, coconut milk and vanilla, and combine, using a fork.

3 Mix all of the other ingredients together in a separate large mixing bowl.

4 Add the wet ingredients to the dry ingredients and mix to combine, using a spoon, working quickly.

5 Spoon the batter into the cupcake cases so that they are about three-quarters full. Bake for about 25 minutes in the preheated oven, until they are golden brown and spring back when lightly pressed. Leave to cool on a wire rack before serving.

Carob has acquired a reputation in recent years for not being delicious, but that's not true! It's a wonderful ingredient to use alongside cacao. It gently sweetens the cacao to produce a smoother, more chocolatey flavour

It's strange, but there seems to be a correlation between people who are vegan and people who like a glass of vodka. Just for fun, I've added vodka to these vegan chocolate cupcakes and they happen to taste wonderful.

There's none of the cream cheese usually used for cupcake toppings for obvious reasons. Instead, the creamy icing has a healthy avocado base, which acts as a fantastic medium for the vodka and vanilla. It's a crowd-pleasing recipe that will win over even the most die-hard fan of unhealthy cupcakes and keep my vodka-loving vegan friends happy and drinking to my health!

Vodka Chocolate Cupcakes

MAKES 12

For the cupcakes:
200g/7oz/1¾ cups plain (all-purpose) flour
150g/5oz/¾ cup date sugar
20g/¾oz/¼ cup cacao powder
5ml/1 tsp bicarbonate of soda (baking soda)
1.5ml/¼ tsp sea salt
75ml/5 tbsp olive oil
15ml/1 tbsp apple cider vinegar
5ml/1 tsp vanilla extract
250ml/8fl oz/1 cup water
50ml/2fl oz/¼ cup vodka

For the icing:
115g/4oz ripe avocado flesh (about 1 avocado)
5ml/1 tsp lemon juice
5ml/1 tsp vodka
2.5ml/½ tsp vanilla extract
225g/8oz/2 cups agave powder
10ml/2 tsp stevia

1 Preheat the oven to 180°C/350°F/ Gas 4. Line a 12-hole cupcake tin or pan with cupcake cases or papers.

2 Sift the flour into a mixing bowl and add the date sugar, cacao powder, bicarbonate of soda and salt. Mix to combine.

3 In a separate bowl, whisk together the olive oil, vinegar, vanilla, water and vodka with an electric whisk on low to medium.

4 Add the flour mixture to the liquid ingredients and continue whisking until smooth and incorporated.

5 Spoon the batter into the cupcake cases so that they are about two-thirds full. Bake for about 10 minutes in the preheated oven, then quickly turn the tin around to ensure the cupcakes are evenly baked.

6 Bake for about 10–15 minutes more, until a skewer inserted in the middle comes out clean. Leave to cool on a wire rack.

7 When the cupcakes are completely cool and ready to serve, make the icing. Put the avocado, lemon juice, vodka and vanilla in a bowl and mash with a fork. Whisk for about 3 minutes using an electric whisk on medium until pale, smooth and creamy.

8 In another bowl, sift the agave powder and stevia together. Little by little, add the agave and stevia to the avocado mixture, whisking after each addition. Using a piping bag or a palette knife, ice the cupcakes before serving.

During the winter months, it's easy to find fresh cranberries. Full of antioxidants, they are almost as high in cancer-fighting phytonutrients as acai berries. Truly a superfood, it's a shame just to make cranberry sauce with them and call it a day. They're delicious, and as versatile as any other little berry. These cupcakes are winter baking at its best, the orange and cranberry flavours complimenting each other and warming the senses, and if needed, this recipe is quick enough to whip up a batch for unexpected guests over the holiday season.

Orange and Cranberry Cupcakes

MAKES 18
225g/8oz/1 cup unsalted butter, at room temperature
65g/2¹⁄₂oz/¹⁄₂ cup coconut crystals
grated rind of 2 oranges, juice of 1
5ml/1 tsp sea salt
50ml/2fl oz/¹⁄₄ cup olive oil
120ml/4fl oz/¹⁄₂ cup maple syrup
400g/14oz/1³⁄₄ cups cream cheese
2 eggs
350g/12oz/3 cups plain (all-purpose) flour
20ml/4 tsp baking powder
350g/12oz/2 cups fresh or frozen cranberries, roughly chopped

1 Preheat the oven to 180°C/350°F/Gas 4. Line two cupcake tins or pans with cupcake cases or papers.

2 Cream the butter and coconut crystals together in a mixing bowl using an electric whisk on medium.

3 Add the orange rind, salt, olive oil, maple syrup and cream cheese and beat with the electric whisk for at least 2 minutes, until creamy and cohesive. Add the eggs, and combine with the whisk on low.

4 Add the orange juice and stir to combine. Fold in the flour and baking powder, and quickly stir in the cranberries.

5 Spoon the batter into the cupcake cases so that they are about three-quarters full and bake for 15–20 minutes, until they are golden brown and spring back when lightly pressed.

Cupcakes, Slices and Scones

Fresh cranberries are one of the most nutritious berries. Full of antioxidants, they are almost as high in cancer-fighting phytonutrients as acai berries

Perhaps the oldest combination in the book, milk and honey seamlessly combine to create a timeless treat. Here they are blended with olive oil to create a rich, dense batter for Spanish-style magdalenas.

They're made with rice flour, which is a traditional flour used in Spanish baking, and also happens to be gluten-free. If you would prefer to use plain flour, simply replace the rice flour, oat flour, and potato starch with the same quantity of plain flour and this recipe will still work perfectly. These are best served fresh on the day they are baked.

Milk and Honey Magdalenas

MAKES 12
50ml/2fl oz/¼ cup olive oil
50ml/2fl oz/¼ cup milk
50ml/2fl oz/¼ cup clear honey, warmed
30g/1¼oz/¼ cup coconut sugar
2.5ml/½ tsp vanilla extract
1 egg
75g/3oz/½ cup rice flour
25g/1oz/¼ cup oat flour
25g/1oz/¼ cup potato starch
25g/1oz/¼ cup ground almonds
10ml/2 tsp baking powder
1.5ml/¼ tsp sea salt

Perhaps the oldest combination in the book, milk and honey seamlessly combine to create a timeless treat

1 Preheat the oven to 180°C/350°F/ Gas 4. Line a 12-hole cupcake tin or pan with cupcake cases or papers.

2 Put the olive oil, milk, honey, coconut sugar, vanilla and egg in a mixing bowl and beat together first with a fork, then with an electric whisk on medium for about 3 minutes.

3 Sift the dry ingredients into a separate bowl.

4 Slowly pour the dry ingredients into the wet ingredients, beating continuously on low to combine.

5 Spoon the batter into the cupcake cases so that they are about three-quarters full. Bake for 18–20 minutes in the preheated oven, until a skewer inserted into the middle comes out clean. Leave to cool in the tin before serving.

These are made with rice flour, which is a traditional flour used in Spanish baking, and also happens to be gluten-free. They are best served fresh on the day they are baked

COOK'S TIP:
Instead of vanilla, add the grated rind of half a lemon, or a quarter of an orange. If you like floral flavours, add a teaspoon of rose water or orange blossom water at this stage, either in addition to the rind, or to replace it.

This is a rustic recipe with autumnal apples suspended in a dense sponge cake. I discovered it in New York, where the locally grown apples are perhaps the best in America due to cold winters and hot summers. Excellent as a dunking companion with a cup of tea, this cake improves the day after it's baked, and just keeps getting better.

When you first stir the mixture, it may seem that there's too much apple, but the chunks reduce in size as it cooks. By the time this cake is baked, it will be the perfect amount. Apples are sometimes tart and sometimes sweet, so adjust the amount of coconut sugar to the apples' natural sweetness, and your own preferences.

Apple Cake Squares

MAKES 9
50g/2oz/$\frac{1}{2}$ cup wholemeal (whole-wheat) flour or spelt flour
150g/5oz/1$\frac{1}{4}$ cups plain (all-purpose) flour
2.5ml/$\frac{1}{2}$ tsp ground cinnamon
5ml/1 tsp bicarbonate of soda (baking soda)
1.5ml/$\frac{1}{4}$ tsp sea salt
115g/4oz/$\frac{1}{2}$ cup unsalted butter, diced, plus extra for greasing
30–65g/1$\frac{1}{4}$–2$\frac{1}{2}$oz/$\frac{1}{4}$–$\frac{1}{2}$ cup coconut sugar
2 eggs, lightly beaten
2 medium apples, unpeeled and chopped into small pieces

1 Preheat the oven to 180°C/350°F/Gas 4. Grease a 20cm x 20cm/8in x 8in square cake tin or pan with oil and line it with baking parchment.

2 Sift the flours, cinnamon, bicarbonate of soda, and salt into a bowl. Discard any pieces of bran left in the sieve or strainer.

3 Melt the butter in a small pan over a very low heat until just liquid, but no more. Pour it into a bowl, add the coconut sugar, stir and set aside.

4 Add the butter mixture to the flour and stir with a wooden spoon until combined. Add the egg and stir again, then quickly stir in the apple pieces.

5 Spoon the batter into the tin and roughly even the surface. Bake the cake in the preheated oven for 25–30 minutes until it is golden brown and springs back when lightly pressed.

6 Remove from the oven, and from the tin, using the parchment paper to lift it out. Cut into 9 squares and serve.

COOK'S TIP
Try replacing the apples with fresh berries in summer or rhubarb in spring. To do this, chop two stalks of rhubarb into small pieces. Cook them in a small, covered pan with 60ml/4 tbsp of honey and a teaspoon of water for about 10 minutes. Add the rhubarb compote to the cake instead of the apple at the end of the preparation steps, and replace the cinnamon with a little freshly grated nutmeg.

It will seem as if there's too much apple, but by the time this cake is baked, it will be the perfect amount

For every recipe I write, and for everything I make, I only ever use good quality salt. By that, I mean natural salt. No kosher salt. No table salt. Just sea salts, unrefined, natural, and organically certified if at all possible. This book is focused on how to avoid refined sugar, but it's worth mentioning sugar's evil twin – refined salt.

It's much simpler to avoid the health pitfalls associated with salt. Use just a little, and make sure the salt you buy is high quality and comes from a natural source. I suggest using flaked salt for this recipe. Any unrefined sea salt will add a uniquely irresistible quality. I love pink Himalayan salt, grey French salt, and your kitchen isn't complete without a box of Maldon salt.

Salted Chocolate Brownies

MAKES 16
175g/6oz/$^3/_4$ cup coconut oil, plus extra for greasing
25g/1oz/$^1/_4$ cup cacao paste or powder
45ml/3 tbsp mesquite powder
275g/10oz/2 cups coconut crystals
7.5ml/1$^1/_2$ tsp vanilla extract
3 eggs, lightly beaten
75g/3oz/$^3/_4$ cup spelt flour
25g/1oz/$^1/_4$ cup ground almonds
2.5ml/$^1/_2$ tsp sea salt

1 Preheat the oven to 180°C/350°F/Gas 4. Grease a 23cm x 23cm/9in x 9in square cake tin or pan with oil and line it with baking parchment.

2 Melt the coconut oil, cacao and mesquite in a large pan over a low heat until liquid and combined. Remove from the heat.

3 Using a hand whisk, beat in the coconut crystals, then the vanilla and eggs, and finally the flour and ground almonds.

4 Pour the batter into the tin, then sprinkle the sea salt on top. Swirl the salt slightly into the surface of the batter using a fork.

5 Bake for about 35 minutes until the outside has totally set, but the middle is still soft, and a skewer inserted into the middle comes out sticky. Remove from the oven, and leave to cool in the tin for about 1 hour.

6 Put the baked brownie in the refrigerator and leave to firm for about 1 hour. Remove from the refrigerator and cut into squares, then serve at room temperature.

I first developed this recipe for a special event I catered for a group of women who are cancer survivors. Eating no-sugar for these courageous women isn't optional. They need to pay attention to what they're eating, but like to smile and enjoy life. They loved these little muffins because the ingredients are healthy enough for them to eat and the taste and texture are equally as good as the sugary treats they can no longer have.

Find freeze-dried blueberries, as they're much closer nutritionally to fresh berries. They're light and dry, reminiscent of popcorn, but when cooked in these muffins, they become juicy. The fresh blueberries become soft and gooey as the muffins bake, so the two different kinds of blueberries add an element of fun.

Pumpkin Blueberry Muffins

MAKES 16

175g/6oz/1 cup quinoa
185g/6¹/₂oz/1¹/₂ cups pumpkin seeds
2.5ml/¹/₂ tsp sea salt
5ml/1 tsp ground cinnamon
10ml/2 tsp bicarbonate of soda (baking soda)
120ml/4fl oz/¹/₂ cup cold water
45ml/3 tbsp pumpkin seed oil
2 eggs
175g/6oz/¹/₂ cup honey
150g/5oz/1¹/₂ cups fresh blueberries (or frozen blueberries if out of season)
50g/2oz/¹/₂ cup freeze-dried blueberries, sugar-free

Blueberries contain a group of phytonutrients that are thought to help protect the body against cancers

1 Preheat the oven to 190°C/375°F/ Gas 5. Line a muffin tin or pan with cupcake cases or papers.

2 Grind the quinoa in a food processor for about 5 minutes. It will become a mixture of fine flour and larger visible pieces of the grain. When it is as fine as it can be processed, tip it into a large bowl.

3 Grind 130g/4¹/₂oz/1 cup of the pumpkin seeds in the food processor for about 1 minute, and add them to the bowl. Mix in the salt, cinnamon and bicarbonate of soda.

4 Put 25g/1oz/¹/₄ cup of the pumpkin seeds, the water and oil in a blender, process to combine, then pour into a separate mixing bowl. Add the eggs and honey to the bowl and mix with a fork.

5 Gently fold in the fresh and dried blueberries, and the remaining 30g/1¹/₄oz/¹/₄ cup whole pumpkin seeds, using a silicone spatula.

6 Stir the wet ingredients into the dry ingredients very quickly to make a loose batter. Don't worry about any lumps, it's more important to work fast.

7 Pour the batter into the muffin cases and bake for 18–25 minutes, until the tops of the muffins are golden brown and a toothpick inserted into the middle comes out clean.

COOK'S TIP
Try this recipe with barley malt syrup instead of the honey for a slightly milder sweetness.

Somewhere between a cookie and a cake, these little treats are fantastic served as they are or coated with sugar-free chocolate. They also make a delicious base for other, more complicated desserts. Crumble them up and add to a trifle, or soak them in coffee and layer them at the bottom of a tiramisu. I've added pine nuts for their oily moisture, and for their delicate flavour, but it's equally possible to replace the pine nuts with dried coconut or cacao powder.

Apparently these humble little cakes were first served in the late 15th century to celebrate the King of France's visit to the court of the Duchy of Savoy in Italy. They are also known as sponge fingers, cat's tongues, and my favourite, boudoir biscuits.

Finger Cakes

MAKES 24
15ml/1 tbsp vegetable oil, for greasing
2 eggs, separated
40g/1½oz/⅓ cup maple sugar
40g/1½oz/⅓ cup plain
   (all-purpose) flour
1.5ml/¼ tsp baking powder
15ml/1 tbsp ground pine nuts

1 Preheat the oven to 200°C/400°F/ Gas 6. Grease a large baking sheet with oil and line it with baking parchment.

2 Beat the egg whites with an electric whisk until they form soft peaks, then add a tablespoon of maple sugar and continue whisking until stiff peaks form.

3 In a separate bowl, add the rest of the maple sugar to the egg yolks and whisk for 4–5 minutes, until very pale and creamy.

4 Fold half the beaten egg whites into the maple and yolk mixture.

5 Sift the flour and baking powder into the bowl, then add the pine nuts.

6 Fold the dry ingredients into the egg mixture gently, using a silicone spatula. Fold in the remaining egg whites, then transfer the batter to a piping or pastry bag.

7 Pipe the batter into 7.5cm/3in fingers. Bake for 8 minutes until golden and puffed up. Leave to cool on the baking sheet, then store in an airtight container, until ready to serve.

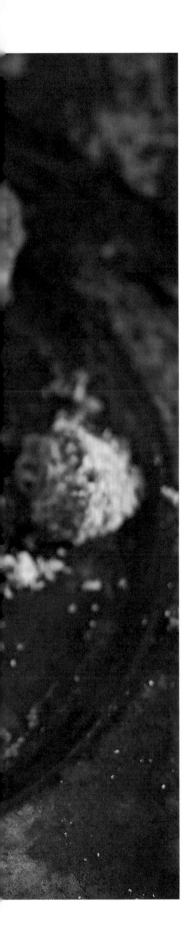

Perfect for teatime or elevenses, these little cakes are delicious and naturally sweet. If you can find it, try using dried coconut that's cut into ribbons instead of finely shredded. As the pieces are bigger, you'll only need to use about half the amount. You can also replace an equal amount of oat flour for the coconut flour if coconut flour is difficult to find.

Coconut and Blueberry Squares

MAKES 9
250g/9oz/2¼ cups coconut flour
20ml/4 tsp baking powder
250g/9oz/scant 1⅓ cups coconut
   crystals
75g/3oz/1 cup dried shredded coconut
   or 50g/2oz/1 cup coconut ribbons
200g/7oz/1 cup cold coconut oil, diced,
   plus 15ml/1 tbsp extra for greasing
2 eggs, beaten
200g/7oz/1½ cups fresh blueberries

1 Preheat the oven to 180°C/350°F/Gas 4. Grease a 20cm x 20cm/8in x 8in square baking tin or pan with coconut oil and line it with baking parchment.

2 Put the coconut flour, baking powder, coconut crystals and shredded coconut in a large bowl and mix to combine. Add the coconut oil, and rub it in with your fingers until only small pea-size pieces remain.

3 Set aside about 250ml/8fl oz/1 cup of the mixture, then stir in the eggs.

4 Pour the batter into the tin and smooth down with your fingers. Drop the blueberries evenly over the surface. Scatter the remaining dry coconut mixture over the top, allowing some of the berries to be left revealed. Pat down quickly, just enough to make contact.

5 Bake for 1 hour–1 hour 20 minutes, until golden brown and a skewer inserted into the middle comes out clean but moistened with crumbs. Leave to cool in the tin, then cut into squares before serving.

Like rock cakes? Well, then you'll love these! They have all of the English tea-party nostalgia of the traditional version, but are sugar-free and low in gluten with a fluffier texture due to the buckwheat. Rock cakes should look like rocks... but they shouldn't be as hard as rocks!

Dried apricots are great in this recipe, but feel free to use any other sugar-free dried fruit. If you're using dried plums or apple rings, chop them coarsely first, but if using dried strawberries, cherries, or blueberries, use them whole. Just make sure you read the packet to check that they're sugar-free, as so much dried fruit is soaked in sugary syrups or even high-fructose corn syrup.

Apricot Rock Cakes

MAKES 10–12

100g/3³⁄₄oz/1 cup dried apricots, chopped
30ml/2 tbsp water
100g/3³⁄₄oz/scant 1 cup spelt flour
100g/3³⁄₄oz/scant 1 cup buckwheat flour
50g/2oz/¹⁄₄ cup erythritol
10ml/2 tsp baking powder
10ml/2 tsp ground vanilla pods (beans) (optional)
2.5ml/¹⁄₂ tsp ground cinnamon
1.5ml/¹⁄₄ tsp sea salt
115g/4oz/¹⁄₂ cup unsalted butter, at room temperature, plus extra for greasing
1 egg, lightly beaten
5–10ml/1–2 tsp almond milk

1 Preheat the oven to 190°C/375°F/Gas 5. Grease a large baking sheet with butter and line it with baking parchment.

2 Put the dried apricots in a small bowl and drizzle with the water. Turn them with your fingers so that they are covered, then set aside to soak.

3 Put the flours, erythritol, baking powder, vanilla, if using, cinnamon and salt in a bowl and mix to combine.

4 Add the butter, and rub it in with your fingers until it resembles breadcrumbs.

5 Mix in the apricots, then add the egg and quickly stir to combine. Add a little almond milk, if needed, to make the dough moist enough to mould.

6 Make little uneven mounds of dough on the baking sheet about the size of fresh apricots, and bake in the preheated oven for 18–20 minutes until firm to the touch. Leave to cool on a wire rack before serving.

COOK'S TIP

This recipe is also wonderful with granulated stevia or granulated monk fruit as a replacement for the erythritol – simply replace it an equal amount of your preferred sweetener. Alternatively, it can be made with 65g/2¹⁄₂oz/¹⁄₂ cup of maple sugar or coconut crystals instead of the amount of erythritol given, and with about 30ml/2 tbsp almond milk added along with the egg if extra moisture is needed.

Rock cakes should look like rocks... but they shouldn't be as hard as rocks!

Here's the news: you don't need to use sugar in scones. In fact, as long as you include the dried fruit and vanilla extract, there's no need to add any other sweeteners. This is a great recipe to start your voyage into sugar-free baking, because it's so simple and quick to make. Teatime just isn't the same without one! Try them either hot from the oven with butter, or cold spread with thick cream and fruit compote, served with a hot cup of tea.

If you can't track down dried mulberries, this recipe works wonderfully with unsweetened dried cherries, dates, or dried plums. They are delicious made with barley flour instead of spelt, but it can be difficult to find.

Mulberry Spelt Scones

MAKES 8
175g/6oz/1½ cups dried mulberries
120ml/4fl oz/½ cup hot tea
150g/5oz/1 cup spelt flour, plus extra for dusting
150g/5oz/1 cup plain (all-purpose) flour, plus extra for dusting
10ml/2 tsp baking powder
2.5ml/½ tsp sea salt
175g/6oz/¾ cup cold unsalted butter, diced, plus extra for greasing
1 egg
10ml/2 tsp vanilla extract
50ml/2fl oz/¼ cup milk, almond milk, or buttermilk

1 Put the dried fruit in a bowl, pour over the tea and set aside to soak.

2 Preheat the oven to 220°C/425°F/ Gas 7. Grease a large baking sheet with butter.

3 Sift the flours, baking powder and salt into a large bowl. Rub the butter quickly and lightly into the flour with your fingers until it is the consistency of breadcrumbs.

4 Drain the dried fruit and discard the liquid. Mix in the mulberries using your fingers.

5 Beat the egg, vanilla and milk together in a small bowl, using a fork. Gradually pour the egg mixture into the flour mixture a little at a time until the dough is very wet and sticky, but is still firm enough to be able to shape. Set aside the remaining egg mixture.

6 Dust the counter with flour, and use your hands to form a flat long rectangle that is about 2.5cm/1in thick and 6cm/2½in wide.

7 For traditional British-style scones, use a round cutter or an American biscuit or cookie cutter to press out 8 scones. For American-style triangular scones, cut the dough in half on the diagonal, and again into quarters, and then on a reverse diagonal cut it into eighths. Pick up each one, and quickly tap the sides down onto the floured counter, so that the sides are evenly dusted with flour.

8 Put the scones on the baking sheet, spaced at least 2.5cm/1in apart, as they will spread when baked. Quickly brush the scones with the remaining egg mixture.

9 Bake for 14–20 minutes in the preheated oven until risen and golden brown. Remove from the oven and serve hot or allow to cool if preferred.

It's strange that regular flapjacks are considered healthy, because nowadays they're usually laden with butter and heavy with golden syrup, treacle or sugar. The same goes for granola. My Granola Flapjacks are a healthy hybrid of these two classics, sweetened with barley malt syrup for malty flavours, and currants for slowly released sugars filled with wholefood goodness, antioxidants and fibre. Sugar-free, gluten-free and vegan, this recipe is as healthy as the flapjacks and granola of your memories. A perfect treat to put in lunch boxes.

Granola Flapjacks

MAKES 18

25ml/1½ tbsp ground flax seeds
75ml/2½fl oz/⅓ cup water
120ml/4fl oz/½ cup sunflower oil, plus extra for greasing
75ml/2½fl oz/⅓ cup barley malt syrup
125g/4¼oz/1½ cups rolled oats
50g/2oz/½ cup chopped walnuts
25g/1oz/¼ cup pumpkin seeds
50g/2oz/½ cup currants
2.5ml/½ tsp baking powder
1.5ml/¼ tsp salt
2.5ml/½ tsp ground cinnamon
1ml/⅛ tsp ground nutmeg
5ml/1 tsp vanilla extract

1 Preheat the oven to 180°C/350°F/Gas 4. Grease a 20cm x 20cm/8in x 8in square cake tin or pan with oil and line it with baking parchment.

2 Put the flax seeds in a large mixing bowl with the water. Mix to combine and set aside to soak.

3 Put half the oats in a food processor and pulverize to make a fine oat flour. Put it in a large mixing bowl with the rest of the oats and all of the dry ingredients.

4 Heat the oil and syrup in a shallow frying pan over a low heat for a couple of minutes to combine. Stir the mixture carefully with a spoon to prevent it from burning and don't allow it to bubble.

5 Gently pour the oil and syrup into the flax and mix in the vanilla.

6 Pour the dry ingredients into the wet ingredients, and stir quickly with a wooden spoon to combine.

7 Pour the mixture into the cake tin, pressing it down to even the surface.

8 Bake in the preheated oven for 25–30 minutes, until the mixture has set and smells wonderful. Allow to cool in the tin before lifting it out using the baking parchment. Cut into bars before serving.

Sugar-free, gluten-free and vegan, this recipe is as healthy as the flapjacks and granola of your memories. A perfect treat to put in lunch boxes

Biscuits, Cookies and Confections

Honey Butter Shortbread, Chocolate Cherry Cookies, Raw Vegan Chocolates, Apricot and Almond Treats... this chapter is packed with cookies and confections that make wonderfully welcoming sweet nothings for guests, as well as tasty little treats to tide you over from meal to meal without any sugary peaks or troughs. All of these recipes have the power to transform the dullest day into an opportunity for pleasure without any guilt!

If you've ever popped round to say hello, you'll remember the little turquoise tin I keep full of chocolates that taste like the moon, but contain no sugar, no dairy... just pure goodness

My no-sugar approach to baking is to embrace the ingredients we use instead of refined sugar, not just because they're healthier, but also because they are more exciting in terms of their unique flavours. In this recipe, ground, dried dates are not only used as a sweetener, but become a featured flavour alongside walnuts – a time-honoured partner in many Middle Eastern and African cuisines. Find ground, dried dates in good health food stores, where they're also sometimes sold under the name 'date sugar'. Alternatively, finely chop dried dates in a food processor. The driest varieties of dates, such as Thoory, work best here, if you can find them.

Date and Walnut Cookies

MAKES 24

115g/4oz/1/2 cup unsalted butter, softened, plus extra for greasing
60g/21/4oz/generous 1/2 cup ground dried dates
1.5ml/1/4 tsp sea salt
2.5ml/1/2 tsp ground cinnamon
50g/2oz/1/3 cup chopped walnuts
50g/2oz/1/2 cup buckwheat flour
50g/2oz/1/2 cup spelt flour

1 Cream the butter with the dates, salt and cinnamon in a bowl, using the back of a spoon. Mix in the walnuts.

2 Sift the flours into a separate bowl, then add to the date and walnut mixture. Mix to form a dough.

3 Bring the dough together, then roll it into a 5cm/2in diameter log. Wrap in clear film or plastic wrap and chill for at least 4 hours, or overnight.

4 Heat the oven to 160°C/325°F/Gas 3, and grease a baking sheet (with sides) with butter.

5 Remove the dough from the refrigerator and slice it into 5mm/1/4in thick cookies. Arrange on the baking sheet about 5cm/2in apart.

6 Bake for 16–20 minutes until golden brown at the edges. Using a metal spatula, immediately remove the warm, soft cookies from the baking sheet and leave to cool on a wire rack.

7 The cookies will become crisp and crumbly as they cool, and will stay fresh for up to 2 weeks if stored in an airtight container.

COOK'S TIP:
The buckwheat flour gives these cookies a wonderful crumb and the spelt flour makes sure they remain intact while being low in gluten. However, the spelt flour can be replaced with the same quantity of wholemeal (whole-wheat) flour, if preferred.

Embrace the ingredients we use instead of refined sugar, not just because they're healthier, but also because they're more exciting in terms of their unique flavours

Moist and sticky, these raw, vegan cookies are gluten-free, dairy-free and so rich that nobody will miss the things that aren't there! Made with yacon syrup, these succulent cookies have a pleasant caramel flavour that's made even creamier with the vanilla. Feel free to fill the thumbprint with any kind of sweet sticky deliciousness such as sugar-free jam, puréed fruit, or a little raw honey or yacon syrup.

I've written this recipe so that you can make these cookies from scratch, but it's also possible to make them with the nut pulp that's left over when you make homemade nut milk. If you are making them from scratch, begin preparing them the day before serving as the nuts need to be soaked overnight.

Raw Thumbprint Cookies

MAKES 20

175g/6oz/1½ cups cashew nut pieces
50g/2oz/½ cup almonds
150g/5oz/1 cup sultanas
   (golden raisins)
115g/4oz/1 cup Brazil nuts
175ml/6fl oz/¾ cup yacon syrup
15ml/1 tbsp vanilla extract
15ml/1 tbsp ground cinnamon
2.5ml/½ tsp sea salt
30ml/2 tbsp oat flour, for dusting
rind and juice of ½ lemon

1 The night before you intend to make these cookies, put the cashew nut pieces and almonds in a bowl and cover with water. Put the sultanas in a separate bowl, cover with water and put both bowls in the refrigerator to soak overnight. The next day, drain the cashew nut pieces and almonds.

2 Put the Brazil nuts in a food processor and pulverize until they are the consistency of flour. Add the drained cashew nut pieces and almonds to the Brazil nuts and continue processing.

3 Add 8 tablespoons of the yacon syrup, vanilla, cinnamon and salt, and pulse to combine into a dough.

4 Dust the counter with oat flour. Divide the dough into about 20 balls, and flatten each one to make cookies that are about 4cm/1½in diameter rounds until all the dough has been used up. Press your thumb into the middle of each cookie to make a large thumbprint.

5 To make the filling, put the lemon rind and juice in a blender. Add the sultanas with their soaking water and the remaining yacon syrup. Blend for about 30 seconds until smooth.

6 Spoon a little of the sultana mixture into the thumbprint in the middle of each of the cookies. Chill for at least 1 hour, or overnight, in the refrigerator, then serve. Eat within 4 days.

COOK'S TIP

To make nut milk, grind soaked nuts of your choice with about four times the volume of water, then strain it through a piece of fine-mesh nylon, muslin or cheesecloth. The liquid is the nut milk, and the solids can be used in this raw thumbprint cookie recipe to replace any of the nuts.

Made with yacon syrup, these succulent cookies have a pleasant caramel flavour

Vegan, sugar-free and gluten-free, these Florentines are thin and crisp with a gorgeous colour. By grinding your own almonds here, the brown skin of the nut is included because unlike store-bought almonds, the almonds you grind have not been blanched. Not only does this mean your cookies have more fibre, it also means the dry mixture is less absorbent, resulting in a much crisper cookie.

If you skip the first step and use store-bought ground almonds, it will still create scrumptious cookies, but a very different kind. They will be smaller and more compact and similar to shortbread in texture. Whichever method you use, the result will be delicious.

Almond Florentines

MAKES 12
200g/7oz/1½ cups raw whole almonds
0.6ml/⅛ tsp sea salt, to taste
1.5ml/¼ tsp bicarbonate of soda (baking soda)
30ml/2 tbsp coconut oil
50ml/2fl oz/¼ cup maple syrup
1.5ml/¼ tsp almond extract

1 Preheat the oven to 160°C/325°F/Gas 3. Lightly grease a baking sheet with oil and line it with baking parchment.

2 Put the almonds in a food processor and pulverize for about 30 seconds, until ground into tiny crumbs.

3 Pour them into a mixing bowl, add the salt and bicarbonate of soda, and mix with a fork.

4 Melt the coconut oil in a small pan over a low heat until liquid. Pour the oil, maple syrup and almond extract into the dry ingredients and stir to combine.

5 Spoon the sticky mixture on to the baking sheet using a teaspoon, and flatten each spoonful into a cookie shape.

6 Bake for 15–16 minutes until golden brown. Leave to cool until hardened on the baking sheet, then transfer to a wire rack to cool completely.

VARIATION
Replace the homemade ground almonds with 175g/6oz/1½ cups of store-bought ground almonds. Leave plenty of space between each cookie, as they will spread as they bake.

Originally a medieval recipe, gingerbread is one of those things that just tastes better sweetened with honey instead of sugar. I've also used ground hazelnuts and spelt flour to create a gingerbread that is as close to the historic recipes as possible. If you want to add a little something extra, add a teaspoon or two of rum. I've omitted it from this recipe for the sake of the children, and because rum is so sweet, but if you're feeling naughty, go for it!

Bake a box of these to give to friends or loved-ones over the holidays, or hang them with ribbons to decorate the Christmas tree. They are best made in advance as the gingerbread is at its most delicious 5–7 days after baking.

Honey Gingerbread Men

MAKES 20
115g/4oz/1 cup hazelnuts
350g/12oz/3 cups spelt flour
15ml/1 tbsp cacao powder
5ml/1 tsp baking powder
15ml/1 tbsp ground ginger
10ml/2 tsp ground cinnamon
5ml/1 tsp grated nutmeg
5ml/1 tsp ground cloves
250ml/8fl oz/1 cup clear honey
1 egg
60ml/4 tbsp raw agave
20 whole almonds, to decorate

1 Put the hazelnuts in a food processor to pulverize, then transfer to a large mixing bowl. Sift most of the flour into the bowl, reserving 60ml/4 tbsp for dusting. Sift in the cacao, baking powder and spices.

2 Warm the honey by standing the jar in a bowl of hot water, then pour it into a small bowl. Add the egg and agave, and gently beat together. Pour the honey and egg mixture into the flour mixture to create a very sticky dough.

3 Cut two pieces of baking parchment to fit a 35cm x 18cm/14in x 7in baking sheet. Put one of the sheets on the counter, and place the dough on top. Dust it with flour, then press the dough with your fingers to flatten.

4 Dust more flour on top of the flattened dough and lay the other sheet of baking parchment on top. Using a rolling pin, roll the dough out so that it's about 5mm/¼in thick.

5 Carefully pick up the whole paper and lay it on a baking sheet. Chill overnight in the refrigerator, or for a minimum of 1 hour.

6 When you're ready to bake, heat the oven to 180°C/350°F/Gas 4. Put a large bowl of hot water in the oven so that it produces some moisture while baking. Remove the sheet of gingerbread dough from the refrigerator and peel off the top layer of paper.

7 Cut out the gingerbread men with a flour-dusted cutter, and add any decorative markings with a knife. If making Christmas tree decorations, poke a hole in the top of each one so that a ribbon can be tied through it.

8 Grease a baking sheet with oil and line it with baking parchment. Put the cookies on the sheet, placing an almond on each of the chests. Wrap their arms around the almond, if liked, and bake for 10–12 minutes. Remove from the oven, lift the baking parchment off the baking sheet and allow to cool on a wire rack. Store in an airtight container.

Biscuits, Cookies and Confections

Quick, gluten-free and extremely delicious, this recipe will make you wonder why you ever made peanut butter cookies any other way. They are so quick, taking only 15 minutes from getting out the mixing bowl to having hot baked cookies! It's the greatest recipe for midnight snacks, surprise guests or instant treats for the kids.

Peanut Butter Cookies

MAKES 12

1 egg, beaten

250g/9oz/1 cup sugar-free peanut butter (creamy or crunchy, to taste)

100g/3¾oz/¾ cup coconut crystals

5ml/1 tsp bicarbonate of soda (baking soda)

1.5ml/¼ tsp sea salt (optional)

2.5ml/½ tsp ground cinnamon (optional)

50g/2oz/½ cup sugar-free dark chocolate chips (optional)

1 Preheat the oven to 180°C/350°F/ Gas 4. Line a baking sheet (with sides) with baking parchment.

2 Put all the ingredients in a mixing bowl and mix well to form a dough, using a wooden spoon.

3 Roll the dough into small balls and flatten each one, working quickly. Put the cookies on the baking sheet, spaced about 5cm/2in apart. Bake for 10–12 minutes, until well risen and brown.

4 Leave to cool on the baking sheet for 5 minutes before transferring to a wire rack to cool completely. The cookies are still soft to the touch after baking, becoming crisper and more crumbly as they cool. Store in an airtight container.

The greatest recipe for midnight snacks, surprise guests or instant treats for the kids

These indulgent cookies are sugar-free, gluten-free and just as chocolately as chocolate chip cookies. They are rich in raw cacao powder, with the added depth of flavour and sweetness of the cherries. Of course, make sure your dried cherries are sugar-free, or if you can't find these, replace them with any other sugar-free dried fruit, like chopped dried figs.

I've suggested using a mixture of brown rice flour, oat flour and potato starch, but if you prefer, replace these three gluten-free ingredients with old-fashioned plain flour to make up the same quantity. Either way, your cookies will have a wonderful crumbly texture, great for dunking in tea.

Chocolate Cherry Cookies

MAKES 36
115g/4oz/½ cup mesquite powder
80g/3¼oz/1 cup cacao powder
225g/8oz/2 cups brown rice flour
115g/4oz/1 cup oat flour
165g/5½oz/1 cup potato starch
10ml/2 tsp cream of tartar
2.5ml/½ tsp baking powder
2.5ml/½ tsp sea salt
225g/8oz/1 cup unsalted
  butter, softened
275g/10oz/2 cups coconut crystals
3 large eggs
50g/2oz/½ cup dried unsweetened
  cherries

1 Preheat the oven to 180°C/350°F/ Gas 4.

2 Sift the mesquite, cacao, rice flour, oat flour, potato starch, cream of tartar, baking powder and salt into a medium bowl.

3 In a separate mixing bowl, beat the butter with the coconut crystals using an electric whisk on high for about 3 minutes, until fluffy.

4 Beat the eggs into the butter mixture one by one with the electric whisk on medium, whisking after each addition to incorporate. Beat the flour mixture into the butter mixture with the whisk on low.

5 Remove the beaters and stir in the dried cherries with a spoon.

6 Roll the cookie dough into golf ball-sized pieces, flatten them, and space them about 2.5cm/1in apart on a baking sheet. Bake for about 15 minutes until set, then leave to cool on a wire rack before serving. Store in an airtight container.

Sometimes, the quest to avoid sugar can lead to creating a recipe that's possibly an improvement on a classic. Scottish shortbread is one of my favourite kinds of biscuit, so it was very exciting to develop a sugar-free version. I have used oat flour to acknowledge its cultural roots, as well as local Scottish heather honey, which perfectly complements the buttery flavour.

If you can find heather honey, it's worth using in this recipe. Alternatively, use another kind of local wildflower honey from your own region. Its delicate flavour will shine in this traditional recipe with a twist, because the honey is definitely a featured taste and isn't lost in the mix.

Honey Butter Shortbread

MAKES 16

115g/4oz/1 cup unsalted butter, at room temperature
50ml/2fl oz/¼ cup heather honey, warmed
50g/2oz/½ cup oat flour, plus extra for dusting
50g/2oz/½ cup plain (all-purpose) flour
1.5ml/¼ tsp bicarbonate of soda (baking soda)
1ml/⅛ tsp Scottish sea salt

1 Line a 20cm x 20cm/8in x 8in square baking tin or pan with baking parchment.

2 Cream the butter and honey together, then sift in the flours, bicarbonate of soda and salt. Mix together with a metal spoon to form a very sticky and wet dough.

3 Put the dough in the baking tin and smooth down as evenly as possible, using the back of a spoon.

4 Dust the surface evenly with the extra oat flour, then press the dough into the bottom of the tin with your fingers, to flatten.

5 Score the surface into four equal parts lengthways and then widthways, to form 16 squares. Put the tin in the refrigerator to chill overnight, or for at least 6 hours.

6 When you're ready to bake the shortbread, heat the oven to 180°C/350°F/Gas 4.

7 Bake for about 12 minutes, or until golden brown. Leave to cool completely in the tin, then rescore along the visible lines to divide into individual shortbread.

I have used oat flour to acknowledge this recipe's cultural roots, as well as local Scottish heather honey, which complements the buttery flavour

These little coconut bites are quick to prepare and great fun to make with kids! The only thing to remember is to roll the mixture into balls before it's hardened, so don't leave it in the refrigerator for too long.

In this recipe, there are three different forms of coconut. Coconut oil can be found in different grades, just like olive oil. The extra virgin coconut oil is the first pressing and a cold pressed extra virgin coconut oil has the strongest coconut flavour. Desiccated coconut can be found in many different cuts, including macaroon cut. If you can find raw unsweetened dried coconut that's macaroon cut, that's perfect, but if not, you can successfully use any kind of unsweetened desiccated coconut.

Raw Coconut Macaroons

MAKES 30
115g/4oz/¹/₂ cup raw coconut oil
275g/10oz/4 cups raw unsweetened desiccated coconut (macaroon cut)
150ml/¹/₄ pint/²/₃ cup raw coconut nectar
unsweetened chocolate, melted, to decorate

1 Put the coconut oil in a heatproof bowl set over a pan of barely simmering water and stir to melt. When liquid, dry the outside of the bowl and put it down on the counter.

2 Add the other ingredients to the melted coconut oil and mix well.

3 Put the bowl in the refrigerator for about 20 minutes, stirring at 5-minute intervals. Remove from the refrigerator when the mixture has stiffened so that it holds together enough to be rolled into a ball.

4 Roll it into 30 balls using your hands, or a small ice cream scoop or a large melon baller. Lay the macaroons on a platter, drizzle with melted chocolate and chill for at least half an hour, or until ready to serve.

I've adapted this from a recipe by my friend Kate Magic, a wonderful raw food expert based in the UK who I've known for many years. It takes 10 minutes to prepare, and only has four ingredients. It's one of my all-time favourites, and the number one recipe that my friends always ask me to make for them. Actually, if I'm honest, it's the one thing in this book that I eat every day.

The reason I eat this chocolate every day is partly because it's so delicious, but mostly because it's so good for you. It's a fantastic balance of healthy fats that will also keep you slim! Mesquite powder helps stabilize blood sugar and staves off cravings; agave adds prebiotic fibre and insulin into your digestive system and cacao contains powerful antioxidants that help balance your mood.

Raw Vegan Chocolates

MAKES A BOX
275g/10oz/1¼ cups raw coconut oil
130g/4½oz/1 cup raw mesquite powder
50g/2oz/¾ cup raw cacao powder
30–60ml/2–4 tbsp raw agave syrup,
    to taste

1 Line a 20cm x 20cm/8in x 8in square cake tin or pan with baking parchment.

2 Put the coconut oil in a mixing bowl set over a bowl of very hot tap water. Stir with a wooden spoon until liquid, then dry the bottom of the mixing bowl and put it on the counter.

3 Sift in the mesquite and cacao powders and add the agave.

4 Stir with a wooden spoon until smooth and combined, with no lumps.

5 Pour the chocolate mixture into the cake tin and chill for about 1 hour, until solid. Slice into chunks using a sharp knife before serving. Store in the refrigerator, but remove 10 minutes before serving, to bring to room temperature.

These little power bars are a healthy version of the store-bought variety that are often laced with sugar. They are perfect for packed lunches, or for a quick boost before a yoga class or hitting the gym.

It's a matter of preference how coarse or fine you make these treats. They're equally delicious and nutritious processed to a smooth consistency or left a little crunchier. Also feel free to play with the amounts of flavourings used, and to add a pinch of something else, like nutmeg or ground vanilla pods.

Served straight from the refrigerator, they're very firm and chewy, but at room temperature, they're soft with a little crunch from the almonds.

Apricot and Almond Treats

MAKES 16
115g/4oz/1 cup raw almonds
65g/2½oz/1 cup dried apricots
65g/2½oz/1 cup stoned (pitted) dates
5ml/1 tsp ground cinnamon
1.5ml/¼ tsp almond extract (optional)

1 Line a 20cm x 20cm/8in x 8in cake tin or pan with baking parchment.

2 Put all the ingredients in a food processor, and pulse until chopped and combined into a paste.

3 Press the paste into the tin, making it as even and compactly spread as possible.

4 Chill in the refrigerator for at least 1 hour, or overnight. Remove the paper from the tin, and cut into 16 bars.

5 Wrap the bars in sweet or candy wrappers and store in an airtight container in the refrigerator, ready to put each one individually into a lunch box.

I'm a huge fan of soaking nuts before eating them. Soaking activates dormant nutrients, and also if the liquid you're soaking them in is tea or apple juice, then the nuts will absorb some of that flavour. This recipe has an interesting texture because the softened nuts are baked to make them crisp, then infused with honey, resulting in a treat that's special and unlike any regular store-bought nut snack. Honey is a classic companion to pistachios in Middle Eastern cuisines, and rosewater is a trusted staple flavour from this region too.

This recipe isn't a traditional one, it's one that I've developed myself. But the flavours are tried and true from the Persian Gulf to North Africa, and remain some of my favourite combinations – subtly fragrant, sweet and nostalgic.

Honeyed Pistachios

MAKES 2 BOWLS

225g/8oz/2 cups shelled raw unsalted pistachios, soaked in water overnight
45ml/3 tbsp honey
30ml/2 tbsp water
15ml/1 tbsp rosewater
15ml/1 tbsp sesame oil
2.5ml/½ tsp ground cardamom
2.5ml/½ tsp ground cinnamon

1 Preheat the oven to 180°C/350°F/ Gas 4. Spread the nuts evenly on a baking sheet (with sides), and bake for 4 minutes. Remove from the oven, stir well with a wooden spoon and return to the oven.

2 Bake for 4–6 minutes more, until they smell wonderful. Remove the nuts from the oven and put them in a large bowl.

3 Put all the other ingredients in a pan over a medium heat and bring to the boil, stirring frequently. Add the nuts, and keep cooking and stirring until the liquid has been absorbed.

4 Spread the nuts out on the baking sheet again, and return to the oven to dry, for about 3 minutes more. Remove them from the oven when they're sticky but not wet, and spread them on a large piece of wax paper to cool. Serve when cool, or store in an airtight container.

Nutritional Notes

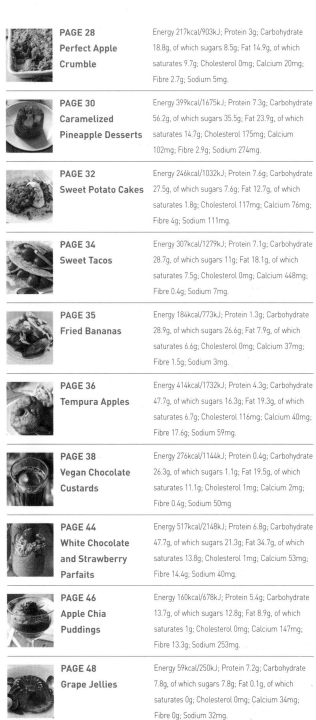

PAGE 28
Perfect Apple Crumble

Energy 217kcal/903kJ; Protein 3g; Carbohydrate 18.8g, of which sugars 8.5g; Fat 14.9g, of which saturates 9.7g; Cholesterol 0mg; Calcium 20mg; Fibre 2.7g; Sodium 5mg.

PAGE 30
Caramelized Pineapple Desserts

Energy 399kcal/1675kJ; Protein 7.3g; Carbohydrate 56.2g, of which sugars 35.5g; Fat 23.9g, of which saturates 14.7g; Cholesterol 175mg; Calcium 102mg; Fibre 2.9g; Sodium 274mg.

PAGE 32
Sweet Potato Cakes

Energy 246kcal/1032kJ; Protein 7.6g; Carbohydrate 27.5g, of which sugars 7.6g; Fat 12.7g, of which saturates 1.8g; Cholesterol 117mg; Calcium 76mg; Fibre 4g; Sodium 111mg.

PAGE 34
Sweet Tacos

Energy 307kcal/1279kJ; Protein 7.1g; Carbohydrate 28.7g, of which sugars 11g; Fat 18.1g, of which saturates 7.5g; Cholesterol 0mg; Calcium 448mg; Fibre 0.4g; Sodium 7mg.

PAGE 35
Fried Bananas

Energy 184kcal/773kJ; Protein 1.3g; Carbohydrate 28.9g, of which sugars 26.6g; Fat 7.9g, of which saturates 6.6g; Cholesterol 0mg; Calcium 37mg; Fibre 1.5g; Sodium 3mg.

PAGE 36
Tempura Apples

Energy 414kcal/1732kJ; Protein 4.3g; Carbohydrate 47.7g, of which sugars 16.3g; Fat 19.3g, of which saturates 6.7g; Cholesterol 116mg; Calcium 40mg; Fibre 17.6g; Sodium 59mg.

PAGE 38
Vegan Chocolate Custards

Energy 276kcal/1144kJ; Protein 0.4g; Carbohydrate 26.3g, of which sugars 1.1g; Fat 19.5g, of which saturates 11.1g; Cholesterol 1mg; Calcium 2mg; Fibre 0.4g; Sodium 50mg

PAGE 44
White Chocolate and Strawberry Parfaits

Energy 517kcal/2148kJ; Protein 6.8g; Carbohydrate 47.7g, of which sugars 21.3g; Fat 34.7g, of which saturates 13.8g; Cholesterol 1mg; Calcium 53mg; Fibre 14.4g; Sodium 40mg.

PAGE 46
Apple Chia Puddings

Energy 160kcal/678kJ; Protein 5.4g; Carbohydrate 13.7g, of which sugars 12.8g; Fat 8.9g, of which saturates 1g; Cholesterol 0mg; Calcium 147mg; Fibre 13.3g; Sodium 253mg.

PAGE 48
Grape Jellies

Energy 59kcal/250kJ; Protein 7.2g; Carbohydrate 7.8g, of which sugars 7.8g; Fat 0.1g, of which saturates 0g; Cholesterol 0mg; Calcium 34mg; Fibre 0g; Sodium 32mg.

PAGE 50
Vegan Strawberry Jellies

Energy 37kcal/153kJ; Protein 0.5g; Carbohydrate 8.8g, of which sugars 8.3g; Fat 0.1g, of which saturates 0g; Cholesterol 0mg; Calcium 19mg; Fibre 1.5g; Sodium 5mg.

PAGE 52
Cold Lemon Custards

Energy 338kcal/1429kJ; Protein 8.1g; Carbohydrate 64.8g, of which sugars 46.4g; Fat 6.8g, of which saturates 3.7g; Cholesterol 75mg; Calcium 186mg; Fibre 3.2g; Sodium 214mg.

PAGE 54
Pear Soufflés

Energy 78kcal/326kJ; Protein 1.7g; Carbohydrate 13.9g, of which sugars 7.5g; Fat 2g, of which saturates 1.3g; Cholesterol 5mg; Calcium 9mg; Fibre 10.1g; Sodium 33mg.

PAGE 56
Zabaglione with Mango

Energy 112kcal/471kJ; Protein 2.5g; Carbohydrate 13.9g, of which sugars 13.8g; Fat 4.2g, of which saturates 1.2g; Cholesterol 151mg; Calcium 23mg; Fibre 1.3g; Sodium 9mg.

PAGE 58
Chocolate Espresso Mousses

Energy 222kcal/917kJ; Protein 4.6g; Carbohydrate 4.3g, of which sugars 1.9g; Fat 20.9g, of which saturates 11.2g; Cholesterol 0mg; Calcium 28mg; Fibre 3.8g; Sodium 103mg.

PAGE 64
Chocolate and Almond Ice Cream

Energy 440kcal/1815kJ; Protein 5g; Carbohydrate 11.3g, of which sugars 2.3g; Fat 41.9g, of which saturates 22.5g; Cholesterol 86mg; Calcium 70mg; Fibre 1.4g; Sodium 95mg.

PAGE 66
Fresh Fig Ice Cream

Energy 408kcal/1697kJ; Protein 4.1g; Carbohydrate 31.4g, of which sugars 31.4g; Fat 30.4g, of which saturates 17.5g; Cholesterol 169mg; Calcium 163mg; Fibre 5.1g; Sodium 47mg.

PAGE 67
Cashew and Almond Ice Cream

Energy 142kcal/591kJ; Protein 4.2g; Carbohydrate 13.6g, of which sugars 13.5g; Fat 9g, of which saturates 1.8g; Cholesterol 0mg; Calcium 7mg; Fibre 2.1g; Sodium 112mg.

PAGE 68
Coconut Berry Popsicles

Energy 11kcal/45kJ; Protein 0.8g; Carbohydrate 1.9g, of which sugars 3.4g; Fat 0g, of which saturates 0g; Cholesterol 0mg; Calcium 5mg; Fibre 1.2g; Sodium 65mg.

PAGE 70
Bitter Orange Popsicles

Energy 15kcal/63kJ; Protein 0.4g; Carbohydrate 4.5g, of which sugars 3.8g; Fat 0g, of which saturates 0g; Cholesterol 0mg; Calcium 15mg; Fibre 0.7g; Sodium 2mg.

PAGE 71
Banana Creamsicles

Energy 49kcal/205kJ; Protein 1.6g; Carbohydrate 7g, of which sugars 2.6g; Fat 2.4g, of which saturates 0.2g; Cholesterol 0mg; Calcium 0mg; Fibre 3.2g; Sodium 19mg.

PAGE 72
Pomegranate Snow Cones

Energy 149kcal/637kJ; Protein 3.3g; Carbohydrate 35.2g, of which sugars 35.2g; Fat 0.5g, of which saturates 0g; Cholesterol 0mg; Calcium 31mg; Fibre 11.3g; Sodium 6mg.

PAGE 78
Chocolate Avocado Cream Tart
Energy 306kcal/1274kJ; Protein 8.5g; Carbohydrate 19.9g, of which sugars 10.9g; Fat 21.9g, of which saturates 5.6g; Cholesterol 0mg; Calcium 38mg; Fibre 6g; Sodium 151mg.

PAGE 80
Cashew Lime Pie
Energy 279kcal/1159kJ; Protein 7.1g; Carbohydrate 12.8g, of which sugars 8.9g; Fat 22.5g, of which saturates 7.6g; Cholesterol 0mg; Calcium 32mg; Fibre 3.2g; Sodium 9mg.

PAGE 82
Coconut Almond Cream Pie
Energy 117kcal/485kJ; Protein 1.8g; Carbohydrate 5.2g, of which sugars 4.1g; Fat 10g, of which saturates 6.2g; Cholesterol 0mg; Calcium 22mg; Fibre 1.7g; Sodium 25mg.

PAGE 84
Pear and Goat's Cheesecake
Energy 308kcal/1278kJ; Protein 6.9g; Carbohydrate 15.9g, of which sugars 15.3g; Fat 24.5g, of which saturates 15g; Cholesterol 110mg; Calcium 80mg; Fibre 1.1g; Sodium 293mg.

PAGE 86
Blueberry Cheesecake
Energy 314kcal/1311kJ; Protein 12.9g; Carbohydrate 26.9g, of which sugars 26.9g; Fat 17.9g, of which saturates 7.1g; Cholesterol 119mg; Calcium 263mg; Fibre 4.5g; Sodium 156mg.

PAGE 88
Peach Tart
Energy 261kcal/1083kJ; Protein 3.9g; Carbohydrate 15.9g, of which sugars 15.8g; Fat 20.6g, of which saturates 11.5g; Cholesterol 0mg; Calcium 24mg; Fibre 3.8g; Sodium 6mg.

PAGE 90
Summer Bakewell Tart
Energy 171kcal/715kJ; Protein 3.3g; Carbohydrate 15.1g, of which sugars 1.5g; Fat 10.8g, of which saturates 3.8g; Cholesterol 14mg; Calcium 32mg; Fibre 1.3g; Sodium 4mg.

PAGE 94
Mississippi Mud Pie
Energy 518kcal/1652kJ; Protein 5g; Carbohydrate 25.4g, of which sugars 11.8g; Fat 34.1g, of which saturates 15.8g; Cholesterol 0mg; Calcium 30mg; Fibre 5.8g; Sodium 88mg.

PAGE 98
Cinnamon Figgy Tart
Energy 639kcal/2682kJ; Protein 7g; Carbohydrate 63g, of which sugars 34.3g; Fat 41.3g, of which saturates 24.6g; Cholesterol 156mg; Calcium 224mg; Fibre 10.4g; Sodium 233mg.

PAGE 102
Pumpkin Pie
Energy 488kcal/2055kJ; Protein 7.4g; Carbohydrate 58.8g, of which sugars 23.3g; Fat 26.4g, of which saturates 12.7g; Cholesterol 135mg; Calcium 142mg; Fibre 4g; Sodium 179mg.

PAGE 106
Cherry Pie
Energy 524kcal/2210kJ; Protein 6.8g; Carbohydrate 69.2g, of which sugars 28.2g; Fat 26.1g, of which saturates 14.2g; Cholesterol 59mg; Calcium 75mg; Fibre 6.3g; Sodium 4mg.

PAGE 114
Christmas Fruit and Nut Cake
Energy 320kcal/1329kJ; Protein 6.7g; Carbohydrate 22.5g, of which sugars 13.3g; Fat 25.6g, of which saturates 13.9g; Cholesterol 58mg; Calcium 91mg; Fibre 3.6g; Sodium 473mg.

PAGE 116
Victoria Sponge Supreme
Energy 724kcal/3008kJ; Protein 10.6g; Carbohydrate 64g, of which sugars 30g; Fat 49.1g, of which saturates 32.6g; Cholesterol 194mg; Calcium 107mg; Fibre 3g; Sodium 475mg.

PAGE 120
Pink Velvet Cake
Energy 327kcal/1369kJ; Protein 9g; Carbohydrate 27.5g, of which sugars 13.9g; Fat 20.7g, of which saturates 8.5g; Cholesterol 88mg; Calcium 131mg; Fibre 3.8g; Sodium 438mg.

PAGE 124
Orange and Almond Cake
Energy 481kcal/1999kJ; Protein 14.4g; Carbohydrate 43.5g, of which sugars 39.4g; Fat 29g, of which saturates 3.1g; Cholesterol 103mg; Calcium 149mg; Fibre 0.8g; Sodium 164mg.

PAGE 126
Vanilla and Chocolate Layer Cake
Energy 494kcal/2053kJ; Protein 8.1g; Carbohydrate 38.8g, of which sugars 11.3g; Fat 38.1g, of which saturates 18.7g; Cholesterol 131mg; Calcium 137mg; Fibre 7.9g; Sodium 727mg.

PAGE 128
Carrot and Apple Cake
Energy 325kcal/1353kJ; Protein 4.8g; Carbohydrate 35.3g, of which sugars 22.8g; Fat 19.3g, of which saturates 10.5g; Cholesterol 39mg; Calcium 53mg; Fibre 4g; Sodium 428mg.

PAGE 130
Flourless Chocolate Roll
Energy 118kcal/491kJ; Protein 4.6g; Carbohydrate 13.3g, of which sugars 11.2g; Fat 5.6g, of which saturates 2.8g; Cholesterol 116mg; Calcium 19mg; Fibre 1.4g; Sodium 73mg.

PAGE 132
Lemon Drizzle Loaf Cake
Energy 430kcal/1799kJ; Protein 8.1g; Carbohydrate 38.5g, of which sugars 27.1g; Fat 28.1g, of which saturates 13.4g; Cholesterol 137mg; Calcium 66mg; Fibre 1.1g; Sodium 83mg.

PAGE 134
Oat Fruit Bread
Energy 265kcal/1122kJ; Protein 5.7g; Carbohydrate 51.7g, of which sugars 30.1g; Fat 5.5g, of which saturates 1.5g; Cholesterol 0mg; Calcium 47mg; Fibre 3.5g; Sodium 526mg.

PAGE 140
Chocolate Banana Cupcakes
Energy 254kcal/1059kJ; Protein 5.8g; Carbohydrate 23.4g, of which sugars 13.5g; Fat 15.8g, of which saturates 3.1g; Cholesterol 0mg; Calcium 31mg; Fibre 5.2g; Sodium 563mg.

PAGE 142
Vodka Chocolate Cupcakes
Energy 203kcal/850kJ; Protein 2.4g; Carbohydrate 31.7g, of which sugars 10.6g; Fat 7.1g, of which saturates 1.3g; Cholesterol 0mg; Calcium 27mg; Fibre 10.3g; Sodium 145mg.

	PAGE 144 Orange and Cranberry Cupcakes	Energy 295kcal/1232kJ; Protein 3.4g; Carbohydrate 22.9g, of which sugars 8g; Fat 22.7g, of which saturates 12.8g; Cholesterol 71mg; Calcium 71mg; Fibre 1.4g; Sodium 213mg.
	PAGE 146 Milk and Honey Magdalenas	Energy 125kcal/522kJ; Protein 2.2g; Carbohydrate 16.9g, of which sugars 6.8g; Fat 5.5g, of which saturates 0.8g; Cholesterol 20mg; Calcium 30mg; Fibre 0.3g; Sodium 137mg.
	PAGE 148 Apple Cake Squares	Energy 217kcal/914kJ; Protein 4.6g; Carbohydrate 25.1g, of which sugars 6.6g; Fat 11.6g, of which saturates 6.6g; Cholesterol 78mg; Calcium 35mg; Fibre 2.3g; Sodium 177mg.
	PAGE 150 Salted Chocolate Brownies	Energy 131kcal/543kJ; Protein 3g; Carbohydrate 18g, of which sugars 12.9g; Fat 10.6g, of which saturates 7.5g; Cholesterol 43mg; Calcium 17mg; Fibre 1.5g; Sodium 134mg.
	PAGE 152 Pumpkin Blueberry Muffins	Energy 173kcal/722kJ; Protein 5.5g; Carbohydrate 16.9g, of which sugars 9.8g; Fat 9.6g, of which saturates 1.5g; Cholesterol 29mg; Calcium 26mg; Fibre 1.4g; Sodium 82mg.
	PAGE 154 Finger Cakes	Energy 29kcal/122kJ; Protein 0.9g; Carbohydrate 3.4g, of which sugars 2g; Fat 1.5g, of which saturates 0.2g; Cholesterol 19mg; Calcium 7mg; Fibre 0.1g; Sodium 8mg.
	PAGE 156 Coconut and Blueberry Squares	Energy 316kcal/1311kJ; Protein 2.1g; Carbohydrate 40.6g, of which sugars 23.7g; Fat 22.8g, of which saturates 19.1g; Cholesterol 51mg; Calcium 42mg; Fibre 14.8g; Sodium 310mg.
	PAGE 158 Apricot Rock Cakes	Energy 146kcal/616kJ; Protein 2.4g; Carbohydrate 16.6g, of which sugars 3.6g; Fat 8.2g, of which saturates 4.8g; Cholesterol 39mg; Calcium 25mg; Fibre 3.5g; Sodium 111mg.
	PAGE 160 Mulberry Spelt Scones	Energy 294kcal/1239kJ; Protein 4.7g; Carbohydrate 31.4g, of which sugars 2.3g; Fat 17.3g, of which saturates 10.3g; Cholesterol 72mg; Calcium 67mg; Fibre 5.4g; Sodium 165mg.
	PAGE 162 Granola Flapjacks	Energy 124kcal/518kJ; Protein 2.2g; Carbohydrate 11.2g, of which sugars 5.6g; Fat 8.1g, of which saturates 0.9g; Cholesterol 0mg; Calcium 10mg; Fibre 1.4g; Sodium 7mg.
	PAGE 168 Date and Walnut Cookies	Energy 82kcal/344kJ; Protein 0.9g; Carbohydrate 8.4g, of which sugars 4.6g; Fat 5.1g, of which saturates 2.5g; Cholesterol 10mg; Calcium 7mg; Fibre 1.2g; Sodium 1mg.
	PAGE 170 Raw Thumbprint Cookies	Energy 131kcal/546kJ; Protein 3.1g; Carbohydrate 12.4g, of which sugars 9.1g; Fat 9.3g, of which saturates 1.9g; Cholesterol 0mg; Calcium 33mg; Fibre 0.9g; Sodium 3mg.
	PAGE 172 Almond Florentines	Energy 137kcal/566kJ; Protein 3.7g; Carbohydrate 4.6g, of which sugars 3.8g; Fat 11.6g, of which saturates 2.4g; Cholesterol 0mg; Calcium 45mg; Fibre 0g; Sodium 3mg.
	PAGE 174 Honey Gingerbread Men	Energy 159kcal/668kJ; Protein 3.3g; Carbohydrate 25.1g, of which sugars 10.1g; Fat 5.8g, of which saturates 0.6g; Cholesterol 12mg; Calcium 38mg; Fibre 3.2g; Sodium 14mg.
	PAGE 176 Peanut Butter Cookies	Energy 137kcal/566kJ; Protein 5.4g; Carbohydrate 9g, of which sugars 7.5g; Fat 11.4g, of which saturates 2.8g; Cholesterol 19mg; Calcium 11mg; Fibre 0g; Sodium 202mg.
	PAGE 178 Chocolate Cherry Cookies	Energy 127kcal/532kJ; Protein 2.5g; Carbohydrate 20.8g, of which sugars 6.9g; Fat 6.1g, of which saturates 3.5g; Cholesterol 36mg; Calcium 10mg; Fibre 2.9g; Sodium 39mg.
	PAGE 180 Honey Butter Shortbread	Energy 81kcal/341kJ; Protein 0.8g; Carbohydrate 6.9g, of which sugars 1.5g; Fat 5.8g, of which saturates 3.4g; Cholesterol 15mg; Calcium 7mg; Fibre 0.5g; Sodium 1mg.
	PAGE 182 Raw Coconut Macaroons	Energy 85kcal/349kJ; Protein 0.3g; Carbohydrate 4.7g, of which sugars 0.8g; Fat 7.3g, of which saturates 6.3g; Cholesterol 0mg; Calcium 1mg; Fibre 1g; Sodium 2mg.
	PAGE 183 Raw Vegan Chocolates	Energy 3195kcal/13189kJ; Protein 27.4g; Carbohydrate 153.7g, of which sugars 36.3g; Fat 282.9g, of which saturates 241.2g; Cholesterol 0mg; Calcium 78mg; Fibre 96.4g; Sodium 636mg.
	PAGE 184 Apricot and Almond Treats	Energy 62kcal/260kJ; Protein 1.8g; Carbohydrate 5.4g, of which sugars 5.2g; Fat 3.9g, of which saturates 0.3g; Cholesterol 0mg; Calcium 26mg; Fibre 0.7g; Sodium 4mg.
	PAGE 185 Honeyed Pistachios	Energy 759kcal/3151kJ; Protein 20.1g; Carbohydrate 37.6g, of which sugars 22.4g; Fat 59.8g, of which saturates 11.5g; Cholesterol 0mg; Calcium 56mg; Fibre 4.8g; Sodium 20mg.

Index

A

agave nectar 16
    chocolate and almond ice cream 65
    coconut almond cream pie 82
    honey gingerbread men 175
    raw vegan chocolates 183
    summer Bakewell tart 90–3
    vegan chocolate custards 38
    victoria sponge supreme 116–19
agave powder 16
    flourless chocolate roll 131
    pear soufflés 54
    vodka chocolate cupcakes 142
almonds
    almond florentines 172
    almond milk 38
    apricot and almond treats 184
    cashew and almond ice cream 67
    cashew lime pie 81
    cherry pie 107–8
    chocolate and almond ice cream 65
    Christmas fruit and nut cake 115
    coconut almond cream pie 82
    honey gingerbread men 175
    lemon drizzle loaf cake 132
    milk and honey magdalenas 146
    orange and almond cake 124
    pink velvet cake 120–3
    raw thumbprint cookies 171
    summer Bakewell tart 90–3
    sweet potato cakes 33
    white chocolate and strawberry parfaits 44
amazake 18
apples
    apple cake squares 149
    apple chia puddings 46
    carrot and apple cake 128
    perfect apple crumble 29
    tempura apples 37
apricot and almond treats 184
apricot rock cakes 158
aspartame 11–12, 16
avocados
    chocolate avocado cream tart 78
    chocolate espresso mousses 58
    vodka chocolate cupcakes 142
    white chocolate and strawberry parfaits 44

B

bananas
    banana creamsicles 71
    chocolate banana cupcakes 141
    fried bananas 35
    oat fruit bread 135
beetroot
    pink velvet cake 120–3
berries
    apple chia puddings 46
    chocolate avocado cream tart 78
    coconut almond cream pie 82
    coconut berry popsicles 68
    coconut berry popsicles 68
bitter orange popsicles 70
black treacle 22
blackstrap molasses 22
blueberries
    blueberry cheesecake 86
    coconut and blueberry squares 157
    pumpkin blueberry muffins 153
    pumpkin blueberry muffins 153
Brazil nuts
    raw thumbprint cookies 171
buckwheat flour
    apricot rock cakes 158
    date and walnut cookies 168
butter
    cherry pie 107–8
    honey butter shortbread 181
    mulberry spelt scones 161
    pumpkin pie 102–4

C

caramelized pineapple desserts 30
cardamom
    coconut almond cream pie 82
    honeyed pistachios 185
carob powder
    chocolate banana cupcakes 141
    flourless chocolate roll 131
carrot and apple cake 128
cashew nuts
    cashew and almond ice cream 67
    cashew lime pie 81
    chocolate avocado cream tart 78
    oat fruit bread 135
    raw thumbprint cookies 171
    white chocolate and strawberry parfaits 44
cheesecake

blueberry cheesecake 86
    pear and goat's cheesecake 85
cherries
    cherry galette 108
    cherry pie 107–8
    chocolate cherry cookies 178
chia seeds
    apple chia puddings 46
chocolate
    chocolate and almond ice cream 65
    chocolate avocado cream tart 78
    chocolate banana cupcakes 141
    chocolate cherry cookies 178
    chocolate espresso mousses 58
    flourless chocolate roll 131
    Mississippi mud pie 94–6
    raw coconut macaroons 182
    salted chocolate brownies 150
    vanilla and chocolate layer cake 127
    vegan chocolate custards 38
    vodka chocolate cupcakes 142
    white chocolate and strawberry parfaits 44
Christmas fruit and nut cake 115
cinnamon
    cinnamon figgy tart 98–101
    honeyed pistachios 185
    peach tart 89
    pumpkin blueberry muffins 153
cloves
    Christmas fruit and nut cake 115
    honey gingerbread men 175
coconut
    coconut almond cream pie 82
    coconut berry popsicles 68
    peach tart 89
    raw coconut macaroons 182
coconut crystals 15
    apple cake squares 149
    caramelized pineapple desserts 30
    Christmas fruit and nut cake 115
    coconut and blueberry squares 157
    flourless chocolate roll 131
    lemon drizzle loaf cake 132
    milk and honey magdalenas 146
    orange and almond cake 124
    orange and cranberry cupcakes 145
    peanut butter cookies 177
    salted chocolate brownies 150
    vanilla and chocolate layer cake 127

victoria sponge supreme 116–19
cold lemon custards 53
cranberries
   orange and cranberry cupcakes 145
cream
   cinnamon figgy tart 98–101
   victoria sponge supreme 116–19
cream cheese
   orange and cranberry cupcakes 145
   pear and goat's cheesecake 85
   vanilla and chocolate layer cake 127

D
dates 14
   apricot and almond treats 184
   blueberry cheesecake 86
   cashew lime pie 81
   chocolate avocado cream tart 78
   coconut almond cream pie 82
   cold lemon custards 53
   date and walnut cookies 168
   peach tart 89
   vodka chocolate cupcakes 142
dextrose 19

E
eggs
   apple cake squares 149
   blueberry cheesecake 86
   chocolate cherry cookies 178
   coconut and blueberry squares 157
   flourless chocolate roll 131
   lemon drizzle loaf cake 132
   pear and goat's cheesecake 85
   salted chocolate brownies 150
   victoria sponge supreme 116–19
erythritol 17
   apricot rock cakes 158
   pink velvet cake 120–3
espresso coffee
   chocolate espresso mousses 58

F
figs
   cinnamon figgy tart 98–101
   fresh fig ice cream 66
finger cakes 154
flourless chocolate roll 131
fresh fig ice cream 66
fried bananas 35
fruit concentrates 22

fruit powders 20–1
fruit syrups 22
fruit, dried 21
   apricot and almond treats 184
   apricot rock cakes 158
   carrot and apple cake 128
   chocolate cherry cookies 178
   Christmas fruit and nut cake 115
   granola flapjacks 162
   oat fruit bread 135
   raw thumbprint cookies 171

G
gingerbread men, honey 175
gluten-free recipes
   almond florentines 172
   chocolate cherry cookies 178
   lemon drizzle loaf cake 132
   oat fruit bread 135
   peach tart 89
   peanut butter cookies 177
   raw thumbprint cookies 171
   summer Bakewell tart 90–3
   vanilla and chocolate layer cake 127
   victoria sponge supreme 116–19
glycerin 18
goat's cheese
   pear and goat's cheesecake 85
goji berries
   Mississippi mud pie 94–6
granola flapjacks 162
grape jellies 49

H
hazelnuts
   honey gingerbread men 175
high fructose corn syrup 21
honey 8, 10, 15–16
   cashew and almond ice cream 67
   chocolate avocado cream tart 78
   cinnamon figgy tart 98–101
   coconut almond cream pie 82
   fresh fig ice cream 66
   fried bananas 35
   honey butter shortbread 181
   honey gingerbread men 175
   honeyed pistachios 185
   milk and honey magdalenas 146
   peach tart 89
   pear and goat's cheesecake 85
   perfect apple crumble 29

pomegranate snow cones 72
pumpkin blueberry muffins 153
pumpkin pie 102–4
zabaglione with mango 57

I
isomalt 17

L
lactitol 17
lemons
   cold lemon custards 53
   lemon drizzle loaf cake 132
limes
   cashew lime pie 81

M
malitol 17
malt syrups 22
   chocolate banana cupcakes 141
   granola flapjacks 162
   oat fruit bread 135
   pomegranate snow cones 72
maltodextrin 19
mango
   zabaglione with mango 57
maple sugar 17
   carrot and apple cake 128
maple syrup 17
   almond florentines 172
   caramelized pineapple desserts 30
   finger cakes 154
   orange and cranberry cupcakes 145
   perfect apple crumble 29
   sweet tacos 34
   vegan strawberry jellies 50
   white chocolate and strawberry parfaits 44
mascarpone
   pear and goat's cheesecake 85
mesquite powder
   chocolate cherry cookies 178
   flourless chocolate roll 131
   raw vegan chocolates 183
   salted chocolate brownies 150
milk
   milk and honey magdalenas 146
   mulberry spelt scones 161
   victoria sponge supreme 116–19
miracle berries 23
Mississippi mud pie 94–6

monk fruit extract 19
    Mississippi mud pie 94–6
mulberry spelt scones 161

N
nutmeg
    granola flapjacks 162
    honey gingerbread men 175
    oat fruit bread 135

O
oats
    chocolate avocado cream tart 78
    Christmas fruit and nut cake 115
    granola flapjacks 162
    oat fruit bread 135
    perfect apple crumble 29
oranges
    bitter orange popsicles 70
    carrot and apple cake 128
    Christmas fruit and nut cake 115
    orange and almond cake 124
    orange and cranberry cupcakes 145
    pear soufflés 54

P
peach tart 89
peanut butter cookies 177
pear and goat's cheesecake 85
pear soufflés 54
perfect apple crumble 29
pine nuts
    finger cakes 154
pineapple
    caramelized pineapple desserts 30
pink velvet cake 120–3
pistachios
    honeyed pistachios 185
polyols 17–18
pomegranate snow cones 72
pumpkin blueberry muffins 153
pumpkin pie 102–4

Q
quinoa
    pumpkin blueberry muffins 153

R
raspberries
    summer Bakewell tart 90–3
raw cane sugar crystals 13

blueberry cheesecake 86
cashew and almond ice cream 67
cherry pie 107–8
raw coconut macaroons 182
raw thumbprint cookies 171
raw vegan chocolates 183
ricotta cheese
    blueberry cheesecake 86

S
salted chocolate brownies 150
spelt flour
    apple cake squares 149
    apricot rock cakes 158
    date and walnut cookies 168
    honey gingerbread men 175
    mulberry spelt scones 161
spices 19
stevia 14
    chocolate espresso mousses 58
    cinnamon figgy tart 98–101
    Mississippi mud pie 94–6
    vodka chocolate cupcakes 142
strawberries
    pink velvet cake 120–3
    sweet tacos 34
    vegan strawberry jellies 50
    victoria sponge supreme 116–19
    white chocolate and strawberry parfaits
        44
sucralose 18
sugar 8
    why go no-sugar? 11–12
sultanas
    carrot and apple cake 128
    oat fruit bread 135
    raw thumbprint cookies 171
summer Bakewell tart 90–3
sweet flours 19
sweet foods 8–10
sweet oils 20
sweet potatoes
    Christmas fruit and nut cake 115
    sweet potato cakes 33
sweet tacos 34
sweeteners 11–12
    no-sugar sweeteners 13–23

T
tacos
    sweet tacos 34

tempura apples 37
tofu
    sweet tacos 34

V
vanilla
    cashew lime pie 81
    cinnamon figgy tart 98–101
    coconut almond cream pie 82
    milk and honey magdalenas 146
    pink velvet cake 120–3
    raw thumbprint cookies 171
    vanilla and chocolate layer cake 127
vegan recipes
    almond florentines 172
    chocolate banana cupcakes 141
    oat fruit bread 135
    raw thumbprint cookies 171
    raw vegan chocolates 183
    vegan chocolate custards 38
    vegan strawberry jellies 50
    vodka chocolate cupcakes 142
victoria sponge supreme 116–19
vodka chocolate cupcakes 142

W
walnuts
    blueberry cheesecake 86
    carrot and apple cake 128
    date and walnut cookies 168
    granola flapjacks 162
    Mississippi mud pie 94–6
white chocolate and strawberry parfaits
    44

Y
yacon powder 19
    carrot and apple cake 128
yacon syrup 19
    bitter orange popsicles 70
    raw thumbprint cookies 171
yogurt
    lemon drizzle loaf cake 132
    vanilla and chocolate layer cake 127

Z
zabaglione with mango 57

Acknowledgements

A Brit based in the USA, Ysanne was born and raised in London before travelling to Los Angeles in 2004 – and stayed for a decade. Currently based in New York, she's bound to return to a rural setting sooner or later, as although adores city living, she keenly remembers the pleasures of picking ripe fruit from the tree and fresh greens from the garden, having managed organic estates and family orchards in the mountains around Malibu and Topanga Canyon. Let's see where her next garden grows...

Ysanne's first book *The Organic Cookbook*, also published by Lorenz Books, sells around the world, and her trove of other books includes *The Ranch Cookbook* for Rizzoli, *Fresh & Wild: A Real Food Adventure* for HarperCollins, and *The Real Taste of Japan* for Clearspring. She has written for the Los Angeles Times Food Section, Observer Food Monthly, and for many leading magazines and newspapers. Her popular blog has been going since 1999 at www.OrganicFoodee.com, and she serves up her own supper club at www.Kindelish.com.

From her edible gardens to her travelling kitchen, Ysanne concocts recipes that deliver the flavours you crave, but with a real understanding of the ingredients at the root of each dish. Herbs, salts and spices are magical powders to add warmth, minerals and exoticism. No-sugar sweeteners are used not just for their sweetening powers, but for their vitamin and enzyme profiles, the tastes they contain, and the colours they impart. The recipes in this book offer everyone healthy indulgence, and taste delicious!

First and foremost, I'd like to thank my friends who've eaten these no-sugar delights. If you've participated in this book as a recipe tester or as a tea party guest, thank you for enjoying these little treats, and for your feedback and happy chomping sounds... If you've eaten sweet things made by my hands, please know that you are dear to me, and I am grateful that our life paths have crossed, if only for a fleeting moment, or for the rest of our lives. What sweetness we shall taste from each other's tables!

In particular, thank you to:
Paul Campbell, Tanya Lam, Charlene Yin, Michael Hochberg, and all my NYC East Village friends, Kindelish guests, birthday party revellers, and willing testers.
Bella Erikson, Stu Robertson, Aasha Robertson, Jodi Wille, Richard Stein, Shaman Durek, and all my Los Angeles family who are so close to my heart, yet as numerous as stars.
Sue and Alex Glasscock, Alexx Guevara, Julia Corbett, Elise Mallove, Leeta Kunnel, and all my Santa Monica Mountain fairies who inspire me every day.
Kate Magic, Terri Wingham, Rawvolution, Café Gratitude, Evan Kleiman, and all of the raw and innovative no-sugar foodies of Venice, California.
And my friends and family in the UK for trying out these recipes, and discovering that no-sugar isn't just sensible, it's fun and delicious!
Lastly, but definitely not least, my heartfelt thanks to Joanna Lorenz for her painstaking attention to detail, her incredible faith, patience, vision, and support for culinary beauty, and to Nicki Dowey, the fabulous food and prop stylists, and Adelle Mahoney the designer. I'm incredibly grateful to the whole production team at Lorenz Books. Thank you!

This edition is published by Lorenz Books, an imprint of Anness Publishing Ltd, 108 Great Russell Street, London WC1B 3NA; info@anness.com

www.lorenzbooks.com; www.annesspublishing.com; twitter: @Anness_Books

If you like the images in this book and would like to investigate using them for publishing, promotions or advertising, please visit our website www.practicalpictures.com for more information.

© Anness Publishing Ltd 2017

A CIP catalogue record for this book is available from the British Library.

Publisher: Joanna Lorenz
Photographer: Nicki Dowey
Food stylists: Annie Rigg and Lucy McElvie
Prop stylist: Wei Tang
Designer: Adelle Mahoney
Text editors: Ellen Sophia Parnavelas
 and Sarah Lumby
For the author picture above left: Tanya Lam, with colour correction by Jason Snyder

COOK'S NOTES

Bracketed terms are intended for American readers. For all recipes, quantities are given in both metric and imperial measures and, where appropriate, in standard cups and spoons. Follow one set of measures, but not a mixture, because they are not interchangeable. Standard spoon and cup measures are level.
1 tsp = 5ml, 1 tbsp = 15ml, 1 cup = 250ml/8fl oz. Australian standard tablespoons are 20ml. Australian readers should use 3 tsp in place of 1 tbsp for measuring small quantities.
American pints are 16fl oz/2 cups. American readers should use 20fl oz/2.5 cups in place of 1 pint when measuring liquids.
Electric oven temperatures in this book are for conventional ovens. When using a fan oven, the temperature will probably need to be reduced by about 10–20°C/20–40°F. Since ovens vary, you should check with your manufacturer's instruction book for guidance. The nutritional analysis given for each recipe is calculated per portion (i.e. serving or item), unless otherwise stated. If the recipe gives a range, such as Serves 4–6, then the nutritional analysis will be for the smaller portion size, i.e. 6 servings. The analysis does not include optional ingredients, such as salt added to taste.
Medium (US large) eggs are used unless otherwise stated.

PUBLISHER'S NOTE

Although the advice and information in this book are believed to be accurate and true at the time of going to press, neither the authors nor the publisher can accept any legal responsibility or liability for any errors or omissions that may have been made nor for any inaccuracies nor for any loss, harm or injury that comes about from following instructions or advice in this book.